US VIRGIN ISLANDS ISLANDS TRAVEL GUIDE 2023

D1216506

Unveiling the beauty of the US Virgin Islands:
Your go-to travel manual for a tropical escape

Ted Paul

TABLE OF CONTENT

Introduction

Welcome to the US Virgin Islands, one of the world's most popular holiday destinations and a true paradise on earth. The US Virgin Islands (USVI) offer an unmatched Caribbean experience that will astound you with its blue waters, white sand beaches, lush vegetation, and rich cultural heritage.

In the USVI, there are many things to do and see for tourists, from visiting historical forts and national parks to snorkeling with sea turtles and indulging in local cuisine. The US Virgin Islands (USVI) are made up of three main islands: St. Croix, St. John, and St. Thomas, each of which has an own personality and allure.

Planning a trip to the USVI, however, can be difficult due to the abundance of possibilities. To help you explore the US Virgin Islands like a local, we've put together this thorough travel guide. This book will provide you all the knowledge you need to enjoy your island holiday, whether you're a seasoned traveler or a first-time visitor.

You can find comprehensive information about each of the USVI islands in our book, including the best places to eat, drink, shop, and stay as well as the top attractions and beaches. Additionally, you'll learn useful travel advice like the best time to go, how to get around, and how to keep safe and healthy.

That's not all, though. Additionally, we'll introduce you to the local food, take you on a tour of USVI culture and history, and give you suggestions for festivals and events. Additionally, if you enjoy being outside, you'll adore our chapter on outdoor activities and water sports, which includes island hopping and touring the many national parks and historic sites.

We give advice on how to be a responsible traveler and support local companies since we think that traveling should be an enriching and sustainable experience.

Join us as we visit the US Virgin Islands and discover the finest of what these stunning islands have to offer, whether you're thinking of a romantic getaway, a family holiday, or an action-packed excursion.

About the US Virgin Islands

A collection of islands in the Caribbean Sea known as the US Virgin Islands are recognized as belonging to the US. Three major islands—St. Croix, St. John, and St. Thomas—as well as a number of smaller islands and cays make up the region. The US Virgin Islands are situated in the eastern Caribbean, west of the British Virgin Islands and just east of Puerto Rico.

The history and culture of the USVI are rich and showcase the region's fusion of African, European, and Caribbean influences. Native Americans lived on the islands at first, but the Spanish, Dutch, French, and Danish later occupied them. Since the US bought the region from Denmark in 1917, tourists have loved visiting the islands.

The three main islands each have its own personality and attraction:

The largest of the three islands, St. Croix, is renowned for its beautiful beaches, sugar cane farms, and old-world architecture. If you want to get away from it all, the island is a perfect choice because of its calm, laid-back environment.

The Virgin Islands National Park, which occupies two-thirds of the island of St. John, is located there and is the smallest of the three islands. Numerous recreational pursuits, such as hiking, snorkeling, and camping, are available in the park. Additionally, St. John is well-known for its stunning beaches and vibrant coral reefs.

The most international of the three islands, St. Thomas is renowned for its food, shopping, and nightlife. There are several historical sites, museums, and art galleries on the island's thriving capital, Charlotte Amalie. St. Thomas is a well-liked location for watersports and boasts a number of fantastic beaches.

The USVI islands have a tropical environment with year-round average temperatures in the mid-70s to mid-80s in addition to their distinctive features. The cuisine on the islands is extremely varied and delectable and includes fresh seafood, regional fruits and vegetables, and Caribbean spices.

In general, travelers seeking a blend of leisure, adventure, and culture will find the US Virgin Islands to be a stunning and fascinating location. We'll assist you in finding the best that the islands have to offer in the chapters that follow.

Getting There and Around

Travelers have a variety of options, making it quite simple to reach the USVI. Most visitors arrive by air, landing at Henry E. Rohlsen Airport in St. Croix or Cyril E. King Airport on St. Thomas. Both airports offer connecting flights from foreign airports as well as direct flights from significant US cities. Travelers can also fly to San Juan, Puerto Rico, and then take a ferry or a short flight to the US Virgin Islands.

You'll need to know how to navigate the US Virgin Islands once you get there. Taxis, rental automobiles, and public transportation are all available on each of the three major islands.

St. Thomas

The most populated of the US Virgin Islands' three major islands, St. Thomas is renowned for its vibrant atmosphere, hopping commercial areas, and stunning beaches. Here are some possibilities for getting to St. Thomas if you're planning a trip:

Taxis:

One of the most well-liked and practical modes of transportation on St. Thomas are taxis. They are widely accessible at the airport and all throughout the island, and can be called or flagged down on the street. The majority of the taxis in St. Thomas are white, have a taxi sign on the roof, and have a taxi license inside.

The government sets the prices, which change based on the location. To avoid any surprises, be careful to clarify the fare with the taxi driver before boarding. Tipping is also accepted and the norm is between 15% and 20%.

For quick excursions or if you want to avoid the trouble of parking and driving, taxis can be a viable alternative. They are also an excellent means of transportation if you intend to indulge in some of the island's many pubs and eateries without having to worry about operating a vehicle while intoxicated.

It's vital to keep in mind that taxi prices to and from the airport are more expensive than those to other locations on the island. The added expense, however, can be justified by the convenience of having a taxi waiting for you at the airport.

Visitors to St. Thomas have the choice between standard taxis and private taxi services, which provide more individualized and adaptable transportation options. Private taxis might be a fantastic alternative if you have a large group or want to tailor your schedule, albeit they are frequently more expensive than standard taxis.

It's crucial to remember that while cabs are a practical way to move around St. Thomas, they can occasionally become congested, especially during the busiest travel season. Plan ahead and leave additional time for transportation if you're traveling during a busy season of the year to avoid missing flights or other appointments.

Overall, for tourists to St. Thomas looking for a dependable and practical means to get around the island, taxis are an excellent alternative. A cab can bring you wherever you're going quickly and easily, whether you're going to the beach, touring Charlotte Amalie's historic quarter, or just taking advantage of the island's numerous bars and restaurants.

Renting a car:
Visitors who want the flexibility to explore the US Virgin Islands at their own pace frequently choose to rent a car there. When renting a car in the USVI, there are a few things to bear in mind.

First of all, travelers from nations where driving is done on the right side may find it difficult to adjust to driving on the left side of the road in the USVI. It's crucial to keep this in mind while considering whether to rent a car and to drive carefully on the islands.

Second, especially during the busiest travel times, rental car prices in the USVI can be quite exorbitant. However, renting a car can be an economical choice if you intend to spend a lot of time visiting the islands or if you're going in a group.

Make sure to look around for the best deals and book early in advance to guarantee availability while renting a car on the USVI. On St. Thomas and St. Croix, as well as in the cities on each of the three main islands, the majority of big automobile rental agencies have offices.

Make sure you comprehend all of the terms and conditions of the rental agreement, including the insurance coverage, any additional costs, and the fuel policy, before renting a vehicle. In general, choosing complete insurance coverage will protect you in the event of an accident or theft.

The roads in the USVI can be narrow and twisty, and some drivers might not be familiar with the routes, so it's crucial to be aware of the local traffic rules and drive defensively. As many roads on the islands are unmarked and can be simple to overlook, be sure to also pay attention to road signs.

Additionally, bear in mind that parking may be scarce in some areas when renting a car on the USVI, particularly in well-known tourist spots like Charlotte Amalie on St. Thomas. Asking your rental car company for parking guidance or doing ahead research on parking choices is an excellent idea.

It's also crucial to be aware that some of the USVI's roads may be unpaved or in bad condition, and others may be winding and narrow. Renting a vehicle with adequate clearance and being ready to navigate imperfect roads are also wise decisions.

Make sure to return your rental car with a full tank of gas when you pick it up, as certain rental car companies may charge extra for refueling the vehicle. In order to prevent any further fines, make sure to return the automobile on schedule as well.

Overall, driving around the US Virgin Islands might be a terrific way to see everything they have to offer. Just remember to make your plans in advance, drive cautiously, and be ready for some particular driving difficulties on the islands.

Public Transportation:
While public transit is also available on all of the major islands, taxis and rental automobiles are the most practical modes of transportation for tourists visiting the USVI. Public buses and safari buses are available on St. Thomas, but service is occasionally sporadic and unreliable.

Safari Buses:
The most popular kind of public transportation on St. Thomas is the safari bus. These open-air vans cover most of the top tourist attractions and are a pleasant and inexpensive way to move across the island. They adhere to predetermined routes. The normal fare is from $1 to $2 per ride, making them an excellent choice for tourists on a limited budget.

Safari buses can, however, be erratic and unreliable. They frequently follow a "island time" schedule, therefore they might not follow a strict schedule. Furthermore, they could be congested during rush hour, and the drivers might not speak English well.

Commuter Buses:
On St. Thomas, there are both public buses and safari buses that operate. These buses frequently feature more space than safari buses and air conditioning, which is helpful given the

island's hot and muggy weather. The usual fare ranges from $1 to $2, which makes them also reasonably priced.

Public buses, however, can be unreliable and may not adhere to a defined timetable, much like safari buses. They might also be less regular than safari buses, so it's crucial to schedule them in advance and allow enough time to travel.

Public transportation can be a good way to move around the USVI if you're on a low budget. However, it's crucial to remember that it might not be the most practical or effective method of transportation, particularly if you're pressed for time or wish to visit several locations in one day. Taxis and rental automobiles are frequently the most practical and dependable solutions for travelers to the USVI, if you can afford them.

If you intend to use the public transportation on St. Thomas, there are a few other considerations in addition to the concerns of dependability and convenience. One crucial thing to keep in mind is that for visitors who are new with the island, the routes and timings of safari buses and regular buses might not be well indicated or understandable. To make sure you know which bus to take and when it will arrive, it's a good idea to seek advice from a local or do some research beforehand.

Despite the fact that public buses and safari buses can transport you to many well-known locations on St. Thomas, they might not be able to take you everywhere you need to go. For instance, you might need to rent a car or hire a private driver to access to some of the island's more isolated beaches or hiking paths.

Despite these difficulties, using public transit can be a terrific way to immerse yourself in the community and get to know some of St. Thomas' warm and inviting residents. Taking a safari bus or a regular bus can be a memorable and entertaining aspect of your trip to the US Virgin Islands if you're prepared for an adventure and don't mind a little bit of uncertainty. Just remember to make a strategy, ask for assistance if necessary, and be ready for a few hiccups along the way.

Private Boat or Charter:
Boaters frequently travel to St. Thomas, and a number of businesses provide visitors with private boat or charter services. If you want to take a day excursion to adjacent islands like St. John or the British Virgin Islands, or if you want to explore the island's numerous coves and beaches, this is a terrific alternative.

Renting a private boat in St. Thomas has a lot of benefits. One benefit is that you are free to explore the island's shoreline at your own speed without worrying about adhering to a timetable or itinerary. A level of seclusion and exclusivity not seen on crowded public beaches can be had by visiting remote coves and beaches that can only be reached by boat.

Several different boat models are available for hire, depending on your needs and financial situation. Popular choices comprise:

Powerboats: If you want to explore the island fast and effectively and cover a lot of ground in a short period of time, powerboats are a terrific alternative. If you enjoy water sports like wakeboarding, tubing, or snorkeling, they're also a wonderful option.

Sailboats: A sailboat can be the best option if you want a more relaxing and intimate experience. While admiring the stunning views of the USVI, you can unwind on the deck and listen to the gentle sound of the wind in the sails.

Catamarans: If you're traveling with a party or family, catamarans are a terrific alternative because they provide lots of space and comfort. They are a fantastic option for inexperienced boaters because they are steady and simple to maneuver.

Do your homework and evaluate costs and amenities before selecting a private boat or charter service. While some charters may charge extra for these services, some may include food and beverages, snorkeling equipment, and other amenities.

You can design your schedule to fit your interests and preferences when you rent a private boat in St. Thomas. Several popular locations are:

St. John: St. John, an island close to St. Thomas, has some of the USVI's most immaculate beaches. By hiring a boat to St. John, you may discover hidden bays and coves and take in the island's famed white sand beaches and crystal-clear blue waters.

The British Virgin Islands: A charter to the British Virgin Islands is a need if you're interested in traveling outside the USVI. The BVI has gorgeous beaches, charming communities, and some of the best snorkeling and diving locations in the Caribbean.

Buck Island is a small island off the coast of St. Thomas that is well-known for its diving and snorkeling opportunities. A protected marine sanctuary is located on the island and is home to a wide variety of vibrant fish and coral.

Make sure to abide by all safety rules and directives when chartering a boat in St. Thomas. This entails donning life jackets and paying attention to the captain's directions. Additionally, it's critical to respect the environment and refrain from endangering marine life or coral reefs.

Overall, renting a private boat in St. Thomas is a memorable adventure that gives you a fresh viewpoint on the USVI. A private boat or charter is a terrific alternative for exploring the island and its surrounds, whether you're looking for adventure, relaxation, or a little of both.
There is a lot to see and do on St. Thomas, regardless of your mode of transportation. The Charlotte Amalie Historic District, the breathtaking Magens Bay Beach, and the beautiful Skyride to Paradise Point, which gives expansive views of the island and the surrounding sea, are just a few of the island's highlights.

St. Croix

The largest of the US Virgin Islands' three major islands, St. Croix, is situated about 40 miles south of St. Thomas. It is the only island in the USVI to have two towns, Christiansted and Frederiksted, and it is twice as big as St. Thomas with a land area of 84 square miles.

The numerous nations that have ruled St. Croix over the years have had a significant impact on the island's rich and distinctive history. During his second voyage to the Americas in 1493, Christopher Columbus arrived on the island and gave it the name Santa Cruz. The Danish West India Company seized possession of the island in 1733 after it had been colonized by the Dutch. The Danish West India Company ruled the island until 1917, when the US bought it from Denmark along with the rest of the USVI.

The architecture, culture, and food of the island are all influenced by its distinctive history. Christiansted, where you may discover quaint, pastel-colored buildings from the 18th century, is where you can really see the Danish influence. The town was formerly a thriving hub of the sugar trade, and the ruins of old plantations like the Estate Whim Plantation Museum still bear witness to the island's sugar plantation heritage.

Additionally, St. Croix has a vibrant cultural history that has been shaped by its African, European, and Caribbean origins. Numerous museums, galleries, and other cultural organizations are located on the island and serve to highlight its rich legacy. For instance, the exhibitions, workshops, and performances that honor the island's arts and culture are held at the Caribbean Museum Center for the Arts in Frederiksted.

St. Croix is renowned for its natural beauty, with lush rainforests, immaculate beaches, and brilliant blue waters, in addition to its rich history and culture. Off the northeast coast of St. Croix, the Buck Island Reef National Monument is a well-liked snorkeling and diving location with a wide diversity of marine life and vibrant coral reefs.

Whether you're interested in history, culture, or outdoor sports, St. Croix is a fascinating location that has something to offer everyone. It is a location in the US Virgin Islands that is genuinely one of a kind due to its distinctive fusion of European, African, and Caribbean elements.

How to Get There

Miami, Atlanta, and Charlotte are among the US cities with direct flights to Henry E. Rohlsen Airport in St. Croix. A quick flight from San Juan, Puerto Rico, to St. Croix is also an option for visitors.

There are ferries running between St. Thomas and St. Croix if you'd rather travel by sea. There are many departures each day, and the ferry voyage lasts roughly two hours.

Getting Around

Taxis: In the US Virgin Islands, taxis are a well-liked and practical method of transportation. They are easily accessible in the main tourist regions as well as at the airports and seaports. Taxis can be flagged down on the street or at designated taxi stops, and they are usually identified by a "Taxi" sign on the roof.

Taxi fares are set by the government and determined by the distance traveled in the US Virgin Islands. At taxi stands and frequently within the vehicles, the latest rates are advertised. It's crucial to remember that taxi fares are negotiable, therefore it makes sense to do so before boarding the vehicle. Prior to beginning your trip, be sure to confirm the entire ticket and any additional charges, such as baggage fees.

Taxis in the US Virgin Islands run on a shared basis, so you might ride along with other people. Given that the fare is shared among the passengers, this is an economical choice, especially for short excursions. If you would rather travel privately, you can order a "charter" or "exclusive" cab, which will transport you where you need to go without making any stops.

Taxi drivers in the USVI are required to display their identification and license inside the car, and taxis are required to have a current license and insurance. Before getting in, it's usually a good idea to make sure the driver has a current license and that the car is in good working order.

If you don't want to rent a car or if you're going in a group, taxis are a terrific way to get around the islands. They provide a practical way to tour the islands and are safe and dependable. Just make sure to haggle the rate and make clear any extra charges prior to boarding to avoid any unpleasant surprises.

Rental cars: If you want to explore the US Virgin Islands at your own pace, renting a car is a popular and practical way to get around. However, prior to renting a vehicle, it's crucial to bear the following in mind:

• To rent a car in the US Virgin Islands, you must be at least 25 years old and possess a current driver's license from your home nation.
• Visitors from nations where driving is done on the right side may find it a little intimidating to drive in the US Virgin Islands because it is done on the left. It is crucial to exercise extra caution and pay strict attention to traffic regulations and road signs.
• Many of the roads in the USVI are steep, winding, and narrow, making them difficult to drive on, especially for inexperienced drivers. Driving should always be done with additional caution, especially at night or in bad weather.
• If you intend to travel to the most inaccessible and mountainous areas of the islands, including the beaches and hiking trails, it is advised that you rent a vehicle with four-wheel drive.

The majority of major vehicle rental businesses, such as Avis, Budget, and Hertz, have locations on the US Virgin Islands. To guarantee availability, it is advised to reserve a rental car in advance, especially during the busiest times of the year.

When renting a car, be sure to thoroughly check the vehicle for any existing damage and, if required, take pictures. Before leaving the rental car lot, you should also check the automobile's fundamental operations, such as the tire pressure and fuel level.

The US Virgin Islands can be explored in great detail by renting a car, which gives you the freedom to go wherever you want, whenever you want. However, it's crucial to be aware of the particular difficulties of driving on the islands and to use extra caution while doing so.

Public Transportation: There are still ways to get around St. Croix if you're visiting and don't want to rent a vehicle. There are alternative ways to go about even if there isn't a public bus system like in St. Thomas and St. John.

Safari buses, commonly referred to as open-air vans or jitneys, are a common mode of public transportation on St. Croix. These automobiles can carry up to 20 passengers and frequently include benches for seats. They travel along well-known routes and can be stopped along the way. Safari buses are an easy and inexpensive method to travel about the island, but keep in mind that they do not always operate on time and may be packed.

Another method for getting around St. Croix is by private shuttle. These are frequently more compact cars that can be rented for a specified day and location. Although private shuttles can cost more than safari buses, they have the advantages of allowing for more privacy and luxury as well as the flexibility to create your own timetable.

On St. Croix, taxis are also accessible and can be located at taxi stands scattered throughout the island or can be hailed on the street. Taxi fares can be negotiated, so do so before you get in the car.

A resort or hotel may provide shuttle services to well-known landmarks or beaches if you are a guest there. Make sure to ask your lodgings if they provide transportation services.

Remember that St. Croix is a relatively tiny island, making traveling about quite simple, no matter whatever method of transportation you select. If you're driving or traveling in a safari bus or shuttle, be cautious to exercise caution because the roads can be congested and twisty. You may simply take advantage of everything St. Croix has to offer with a little preparation and adaptability.

St. John

St. John is a beautiful island in the US Virgin Islands that has gained popularity as a retreat spot for tourists looking for a relaxed tropical vacation. St. John has some of the most magnificent natural landscapes in the Caribbean, despite being the smallest of the USVI's three main islands. The island is the perfect getaway for nature lovers and outdoor enthusiasts because to its stunning beaches, clear waterways, and rich vegetation.

The Virgin Islands National Park, which occupies more than two-thirds of the island, is one of St. John's primary attractions. The island's natural resources and cultural legacy are preserved by the park, which was established in 1956. It features kilometers of unspoiled beaches, coral reefs, and tropical woods in addition to archeological remains and historic sites from the island's colonial past.

The park's numerous hiking paths provide access to breathtaking views of the island's bays, forests, and coastline for visitors to St. John. The Reef Bay path, which travels through the park's tropical rainforest and ends with the remnants of a 19th-century sugar plantation, is the most well-known path. Hikers may encounter local fauna such as iguanas, tree frogs, and tropical birds along the path.

St. John provides a variety of outdoor pursuits and watersports in addition to hiking. Visitors can go kayaking or stand-up paddleboarding in the tranquil bays and coves or snorkeling or scuba diving to discover the island's spectacular coral reefs and underwater animals. Additionally, there are options for windsurfing, sailing, and fishing.

St. John offers a thriving local culture and a laid-back island attitude in addition to its natural charms. Cruz Bay, the island's largest settlement, has a wide selection of eateries, pubs, and shops in addition to a busy ferry terminal that connects the island to St. Thomas and St. Croix. The numerous historical sites and cultural landmarks on the island, like the Cinnamon Bay Plantation and the Annaberg Sugar Plantation, are also open to visitors.

For anyone looking for a tropical getaway that blends unspoiled nature, outdoor adventure, and island charm, St. John is a must-visit location. The island is a wonderful paradise that has plenty to offer everyone with its gorgeous beaches, blue oceans, and lush flora.

Getting to St. John
Only ferries from the neighboring islands of St. Thomas and St. Croix can travel to St. John. The Cyril E. King Airport in St. Thomas, which offers direct flights from a number of significant U.S. cities, is where the majority of visitors to St. John arrive.

St. John is one of the USVI's most picturesque and secluded islands, and its isolation further heightens its appeal. St. John, which is only reachable by ferry from the nearby islands of St. Thomas and St. Croix, provides a genuine getaway from the rush and bustle of daily life.

The bulk of people to St. John arrive via the Cyril E. King Airport in St. Thomas, which serves as the primary entry point for tourists entering the US Virgin Islands. Major airlines like American Airlines, Delta, United, and JetBlue offer direct flights to the airport from many significant U.S. cities like New York, Miami, Boston, and Atlanta.

You may simply take a taxi or a rental car from the airport to either of the two ferry terminals that serve St. John: Red Hook or Charlotte Amalie. While Charlotte Amalie is situated in the heart of Charlotte Amalie and is only a 10-minute drive from the airport, Red Hook is situated on the east coast of St. Thomas.

A quick and simple way to get to the island is by taking the ferry from St. Thomas to St. John. With daily departures between St. Thomas and St. John, visitors have a selection of many ferry operators to choose from. Depending on the ferry company and route, the trip takes 20 to 30 minutes.

Alternative transportation options include taking a ferry from St. Croix to St. John, though these may be less dependable and available less frequently. It takes around 2.5 hours to get from St. Croix to St. John by boat; if the schedule conflicts with your trip plans, you might need to spend the night on St. Croix.

From St. Thomas

Most flights from the continental United States land at St. Thomas' Cyril E. King Airport, which serves as the main entrance point for tourists to the US Virgin Islands. Visitors can then take a bus, taxi, or rent a car to one of two ferry terminals to travel to St. John:

Approximately a 30-minute drive from the airport, the Red Hook Ferry Terminal is situated on the eastern side of St.

Thomas. As ferries run hourly between Red Hook and Cruz Bay, the main town on St. John, this is the busiest and most convenient ferry station for tourists visiting St. John. Red Hook's first and final ferries of the day leave at 6:30 am and 11:00 pm, respectively. The ferry timetable should be checked in advance as it can change depending on the season.

Taxis and automobile rental agencies are easily accessible at the airport, making it simple for visitors to get to the Red Hook ferry station. For those who decide to drive themselves, the terminal has plenty of parking space available.

The Charlotte Amalie Ferry Terminal is a 10-minute drive from the airport and is situated in the center of Charlotte Amalie. Although less frequent than those from Red Hook, ferries from this terminal provide a more picturesque journey through the bay. Cruz Bay is reached by ferry from Charlotte Amalie in about 45 minutes. To get to the ferry terminal, guests can either park in one of the neighboring parking garages or take a cab or rent a car.

Visitors can purchase tickets for the boat voyage to St. John at the ticket booths located in both ferry terminals. Depending on the ferry company and route, the trip from St. Thomas to St. John takes 20 to 30 minutes. The public boat system, which is the least expensive alternative, and private ferry firms, which provide faster and more opulent service, are both available to customers.

There are numerous transportation alternatives available to fit any budget or preference, making traveling to St. John from St. Thomas a very simple and quick affair.

From St. Croix

Even though there is less frequent ferry service between St. Croix and St. John than between St. Thomas, it can still be a good alternative for tourists who want to avoid the crowds and activity of St. Thomas. Depending on the operator and route, the ferry trip from St. Croix to St. John lasts roughly 2.5 hours.

Operating between St. Croix and St. John are two ferry companies:

The village of Christiansted on St. Croix and Cruz Bay on St. John are connected by a once-daily ferry service that is provided by the transportation services of St. John. At 8:30 in the morning and 4:30 in the afternoon, the boat leaves St. Croix for the return trip. A one-way ticket costs $85 per person.

Inter-Island Excursions: Provides a more flexible ferry service between St. Croix and St. John, leaving from both Frederiksted and Christiansted on St. Croix and arriving at both Cruz Bay and Coral Bay on St. John. Check the webpage for the most recent departure times as the itinerary changes depending on the season. A one-way ticket costs $70 per person.

It's crucial to remember that, depending on the weather and other variables, the ferry service from St. Croix to St. John can be less dependable than the one from St. Thomas. It is advised that travelers who intend to ride the ferry from St. Croix to St. John leave some room for flexibility in their plans and be ready for cancellations or delays.

Bring lots of water and snacks for the lengthy trip if you plan to ride the ferry from St. Croix to St. John. On the ferry, you may see peeks of adjacent islands like St. Thomas and St. John in addition to the breathtaking scenery. When you get to Cruz Bay, you can take advantage of everything St. John has to offer, including its gorgeous beaches, lush hiking trails, and dynamic local culture.

Getting Around St. John

There are various ways to move about the island of St. John after you reach there:

Taxis

For visitors visiting St. John, taxis are a convenient and dependable method of transportation. Taxis can take you to the island's beaches, hiking trails, and other attractions, and they are widely available at the ferry dock and across the island.

The government in the USVI sets the taxi fares, so guests can anticipate paying a reasonable fare for their transportation. Before boarding the taxi, it's a good idea to ask the driver for an estimated fare because rates vary based on the destination.

The majority of taxi drivers on St. John are amiable and informed about the island, and most taxis are secure and well-maintained. They can provide you advice on where to dine, shop, and explore, as well as a quick rundown of the island's history and culture.

On St. John, taxis are often minivans or SUVs with enough for up to six passengers. For small parties or families who want to travel together, they are a fantastic option. A terrific way to view the attractions and discover more about St. John's history and culture is to take one of the personalized tours of the island that some taxi drivers also provide.

In general, taking a taxi is a practical and reasonably priced method to move around St. John, especially if you're not used to driving on the left side of the road or don't want to worry about parking. Before boarding the cab, make sure to clarify the fee with the driver, and don't be afraid to ask for advice or suggestions on what to see and do on the island.

Car rentals

Visitors to St. John who wish to explore the island's numerous beaches, hiking trails, and picturesque roadways frequently choose to rent a car. Both in town and at the Cruz Bay ferry terminal, there are various dependable rental vehicle businesses from which to select.

A visitor from a country where driving is done on the right side of the road may find it challenging to adjust to driving on the left side of the road in the US Virgin Islands. However, St. John's roads are generally well-kept and simple to use, and there is a ton ofsignage to direct you in the right direction.

When renting a vehicle, make sure to carefully read the rental agreement and ask any questions you may have regarding insurance coverage, fuel policies, and other terms and conditions. Be cautious to check these information before making your reservation as certain rental companies may have a minimum age requirement or additional costs for drivers younger than 25.

Parking is a crucial factor to take into account when renting a car in St. John. Finding a location to park your rental car on the island might be difficult, particularly during high season, due to the island's constrained parking and tiny roadways. To ensure you can locate a parking space, it is advisable to plan ahead and come early to popular locations like beaches and hiking trails.

Despite these difficulties, renting a car is still a fantastic choice for those who desire the independence and flexibility to explore St. John at their own pace. You can easily get to some of the island's more secluded beaches and scenic areas with a rental car, and you can take your time taking in everything that this lovely island has to offer.

Public Transportation

On St. John, open-air trucks called "safaris" serve as the primary mode of public transportation. These trucks, which have a capacity of 20 passengers, are a well-liked and inexpensive way to get across the island. The east end of St. John (Coral Bay) and the beaches along the north shore are covered by the safari routes.

Safari Routes

A meandering road traverses the island's rugged terrain on the safari route to Coral Bay, providing breath-taking vistas of the Caribbean Sea all along the way. Along the island's main road, there are stops at well-known beaches such Trunk Bay, Cinnamon Bay, and Maho Bay along the trip to the north coast beaches.

Safari Fares and Schedules

The VI government sets the prices for safaris, and they are relatively affordable. You'll need exact change, so make sure you pack some coins and tiny dollars. The safaris follow a regular timetable, with more frequent service from December to April when demand is highest. For the most recent information, speak with the management of your hotel or villa or check the schedule at the Cruz Bay safari stand.

Benefits of Taking a Safari

A excellent way to see St. John on a budget is to go on a safari. Along the journey, you'll get to interact with other travelers and experience the island's breathtaking beauty up close. Additionally, the safaris' open-air layout enables you to travel while taking in the crisp air and pleasant sunshine.

Tips for Taking a Safari

• Be ready for a rough ride! Hold on tight because the roads of St. John may be incredibly twisty and steep.

• Don't forget to bring drink, a hat, and sunscreen. You should drink enough of water because the Caribbean sun can be very strong.

• Don't be hesitant to start up a discussion with other travelers. On a safari, you never know who you'll run into!

• Show courtesy to other passengers as well as the driver. Safaris are shared vehicles, so be considerate to other passengers and pay attention to the driver's directions.

Bicycle Rentals

Renting a bicycle in St. John is a terrific choice for those looking for an eco-friendly and more active way to see the island. St. John is a great area to explore by bike thanks to its beautiful roads, rugged topography, and plethora of trails.

The major town on the island, Cruz Bay, offers a number of rental businesses where you may rent bicycles. The rental stores include many bike types, such as road bikes, hybrid cycles, and mountain bikes, in addition to helmets and other accessories. Depending on the type of bike and length of the rental, daily charges for rentals range from $20 to $40.

The numerous trails and scenic pathways on the island can be explored once you have your bike. The Johnny Horn Trail, Caneel Bay Trail, and Reef Bay Trail are just a few of the pathways that are particularly well-liked by cyclists. The island's fauna, lush foliage, and coastline are all beautifully viewed from these routes.

St. John's picturesque routes provide enough of opportunities to explore the island's numerous beaches, historic monuments, and quaint towns for those who like to stick to the roadways. Popular roads include the Centerline Road, which travels through the center of the island and provides panoramic views of the surrounding hills, and the North Shore Road, which follows the island's gorgeous north coast.

Cycling is a wonderful opportunity to take in St. John's natural beauty and local culture while simultaneously exercising and getting some fresh air. Just remember to pack lots of water, wear sunscreen and safety gear, and keep an eye out for other automobiles and trucks on the highways.

Boat Rentals
Visitors who want to explore St. John's stunning waterways and quiet bays should consider renting a boat. Powerboat and sailboat rentals are provided by a number of businesses, including Island Adventure Tours, Low Key Watersports, and Captain Joe's Boat Rentals.

Visitors who want to quickly and easily explore the island's shores should use powerboats. They are fantastic for beach and island hopping, as well as snorkeling adventures. Powerboats have a maximum capacity of six passengers and come with a number of amenities, such as GPS, safety gear, and snorkeling gear.

For visitors who prefer a more leisurely and conventional method of exploring the island's seas, sailboats are the best option. Up to six people can travel on a sailboat, which has a captain who can lead tourists to the greatest snorkeling locations, secret coves, and undiscovered beaches.

Visitors who want to explore the island's waterways with a knowledgeable guide often choose guided tours. Guided snorkeling trips, sunset cruises, and dolphin-watching excursions are all provided by various businesses. These excursions are a wonderful way to meet other tourists and learn about the island's history, culture, and marine life.

When hiring a boat, it's crucial to pick a reliable firm that has a solid safety record, provides high-quality gear and services, and has a decent safety record. Before you head off, be careful to enquire about safety gear like life jackets and emergency flares and become acquainted with the boat's features and functioning.

Renting a boat is a fantastic opportunity to explore the island's stunning seas and take in St. John's natural splendor. Renting a boat is an unforgettable way to explore the US Virgin Islands, whether you're searching for a romantic sunset cruise or an exhilarating snorkeling trip.

You will undoubtedly be enchanted by St. John's natural beauty, laid-back atmosphere, and welcoming natives no matter how you decide to get around the island.

The USVI is a manageable and generally small destination, making travelling around there simple. Just make sure to prepare ahead of time and select the best mode of transportation for you.

Best Time to Visit

Due to its warm, bright weather, tourists can visit the US Virgin Islands all year round. Throughout the year, temperatures normally vary from the mid-70s to the mid-80s Fahrenheit (about 24 to 30 °C), with sporadic showers and humidity. When preparing for your vacation to the USVI, there are a few things to keep in mind.

Events and Activities:

Numerous annual festivals and events are held on the US Virgin Islands, which can be a big draw for tourists. One of the major festivals of the year, the St. Thomas Carnival, for instance, spans several weeks and features parades, cuisine, music, and other celebrations. The Virgin Islands Food and Wine Festival, the Crucian Christmas Festival in St. Croix, and the St. John Festival are some further noteworthy occasions.

The season you go can also matter if you're interested in outdoor pursuits like fishing, scuba diving, or snorkeling. While the waters surrounding the USVI are always warm and clean, some fish species may be more common during particular times of the year. For instance, the optimum season for deep-sea fishing for species like marlin is winter, whereas tuna and wahoo may be easier to catch in the summer and fall.

Budget:

Depending on the time of year you visit the USVI, travel prices can vary significantly. Peak season, from mid-December to mid-April, is often the most expensive time to travel due to higher costs for airfare, lodging, and activities. If you're ready to be flexible with your trip dates and accommodations, off-season (mid-April through mid-December) and shoulder season (April to early June and November to mid-December) may present more cheap possibilities.

Keep in mind that because the USVI is an American territory, US dollars are the preferred method of payment. Travel expenses for visitors from other countries may increase as a result, especially if the US dollar is strong relative to your own currency. Before your vacation, you might want to think about exchanging money or using a credit card with no foreign transaction fees.

Weather:

The US Virgin Islands get year-round warm and sunny weather, with typical highs in the mid-70s to mid-80s Fahrenheit. Nevertheless, there can be some differences based on the season you visit. The summer months (June through August) can be hot and muggy, with sporadic showers of rain and the potential for hurricanes or tropical storms. With milder temperatures and low humidity, winter (December through February) is often the driest and most comfortable season.

Be mindful that some outdoor activities, such as hiking or snorkeling, may be more comfortable at particular times of the year if you're arranging them. For instance, hiking may be more bearable during the milder months of December through February than during the sweltering summer. Similar to this, diving and snorkeling could be more pleasurable in the drier winter and early spring, when visibility is frequently at its peak.

When organizing a trip to the US Virgin Islands, there are numerous things to take into account. You can select the ideal season to go and take advantage of everything these lovely islands have to offer by taking into account your schedule, hobbies, and other factors.

Why Visit the US Virgin Islands?

Beautiful Beaches: The US Virgin Islands are home to some of the world's most exquisite beaches. The beaches are ideal for aquatic activities including snorkeling, diving, and paddleboarding as well as swimming and tanning. Magens Bay Beach in St. Thomas, Trunk Bay Beach in St. John, and Sandy Point Beach in St. Croix are a few of the most well-liked beaches.

Rich Cultural past: The architecture, music, and cuisine of the US Virgin Islands all showcase the islands' rich cultural past. Visitors can tour ancient structures including Charlotte Amalie's Fort Christian and Government House, both of which date back to the 17th century. They can also enjoy local specialties like conch fritters and johnnycakes while listening to steel drum music, a style of music that has its roots in the Caribbean.

Outdoor Activities: The US Virgin Islands are a fantastic vacation spot for nature lovers. Hiking on one of the many nature routes, such as the Lind Point Trail in St. John, allows visitors to experience the island's beautiful rainforests. They can also kayak across the clear seas of St. Thomas or St. Croix's mangrove woods. Additionally, guests can go snorkeling or scuba diving at well-known locations like Buck Island Reef National Monument in St. Croix to explore a lively underwater environment.

Festivals & Events: The US Virgin Islands host a range of annual festivals and events that honor everything from history and culture to food and music. There are many activities to choose from, but St. Thomas' annual Carnival celebration is the biggest and most well-liked. The St. John Festival, for instance, takes place in June and includes musical, gastronomic, and cultural events, while the St. Croix Food and Wine Experience, held in April, is a culinary event that brings together regional and international chefs.

Ecotourism: The US Virgin Islands are dedicated to developing ecotourism and safeguarding their natural resources. Visitors can take part in eco-friendly excursions like tours of sustainable farms and turtle and bird viewing. Visitors can explore Ridge to Reef Farm in St. Croix, for instance, which supports sustainable agricultural methods and offers fresh fruit to nearby eateries.

Locals are friendly: Residents of the US Virgin Islands are renowned for their cordial hospitality and outgoing personalities. In this lovely and pleasant location, guests may anticipate being welcomed with open arms and feeling at home. The inhabitants take pride in their neighborhood and island home and are happy to share their culture and history with guests.

Shopping: With a vast variety of unusual goods and mementos to choose from, the US Virgin Islands are a shopper's delight. Visitors can look through jewelry manufactured with stones found nearby, such as larimar and amber, or purchase handmade goods like ceramics and woven baskets. Visitors can also find one-of-a-kind treasures in the many local markets and stores to browse.

History and Museums: The indigenous tribes who first inhabited the US Virgin Islands left behind a rich historical legacy. By visiting museums that highlight the art and culture of the Caribbean, such as the Caribbean Museum Center for the Arts in St. Croix, visitors can learn more about this heritage. A look into the island's colonial past is provided by historical places like the Estate Whim Plantation Museum, which visitors can explore.

Nightlife: There are many pubs, clubs, and restaurants to select from in the US Virgin Islands' thriving nighttime scene. The well-known "painkiller" cocktail, which is mixed with rum, pineapple juice, orange juice, and coconut cream, is one of the regional libations that tourists can try. A peaceful supper with a sunset view is also an option, as is dancing the night away to Caribbean music.

Luxury Resorts: The US Virgin Islands are home to a number of opulent resorts that provide top-notch facilities and services. With spa services, exclusive beach access, and gourmet cuisine, visitors may experience the pinnacle of pampering and relaxation. The Ritz-Carlton in St. Thomas and The Buccaneer on St. Croix are two of the most well-known resorts.

The US Virgin Islands provide a distinctive fusion of scenic beauty, a storied past and vibrant culture, outdoor pursuits, celebrations, and opulent resorts. In addition to learning about the island's history and taking advantage of its contemporary conveniences, visitors can explore the island's pristine beaches, rich jungles, and fascinating undersea environment. It's no surprise that people from all over the world choose to visit the US Virgin Islands given the friendly and inviting locals there.

Essential Travel Tips

There are a few things you should keep in mind both before and during your trip to the USVI if you want to get the most out of it. The following are important travel advice:

Pack appropriately:

The US Virgin Islands have a tropical climate, with average highs and lows of 75–85°F (24–29°C). Particularly in the summer, the humidity can amplify the feeling of heat. Packing breathable, light clothing made of natural fibers like cotton or linen is essential. Additionally, you should pack a hat to shield your face from the sun and a pair of suitable walking or hiking shoes. Pack swimsuit, snorkeling equipment, and water shoes if you intend to spend time in the water. Last but not least, remember to bring high-SPF sunscreen and insect repellent to shield your skin from the sun and pesky insects.

Bring a valid passport:

Despite the fact that the US Virgin Islands are US territory, entry requires a passport that is still in good standing. Both US citizens and foreign nationals are affected by this. If you are a US citizen, you do not require a visa or any other travel documentation; however, non-US nationals might need a visa or other travel documents, so be sure to check with the USVI embassy in your country before you travel.

Learn about local customs:

The USVI boasts a distinctive fusion of cultures, including contributions from the Caribbean, Europe, and Africa. Spend some time learning about regional traditions and customs to gain a deeper understanding of the community. For instance, many locals speak the Creole language, so learning a few basic phrases will really help you get along with others. A significant component of the culture is music, and you can frequently encounter reggae, calypso, and steelpan music being performed live in public spaces.

Stay safe:

Despite the fact that the USVI is a typically safe place to visit, you should nevertheless take security measures to safeguard your personal goods and yourself. Keep your valuables and critical papers in a secure location at all times, and stay away from walking alone in desolate locations, especially at night. Make sure to drive carefully and wear a helmet if you intend to rent a vehicle, such as a scooter. Additionally, if you intend to participate in any water sports, follow all safety precautions and carry a life jacket.

Eat some local food:

The US Virgin Islands are renowned for their delectable indigenous food, which combines Caribbean, European, and African ingredients. Fresh seafood like mahi-mahi and snapper, as well as johnnycakes and conch fritters, are some of the most well-liked delicacies. A wide number of rum drinks are also available, including the well-known Painkiller, which is created with rum, coconut cream, pineapple and orange juice, as well as grated nutmeg. While you're in the USVI, be sure to sample some regional cuisine!

Respect the environment:

In the USVI, you may find some of the most breathtaking natural settings in the Caribbean, such as unspoiled beaches, coral reefs, and lush jungles. Doing your part to protect the environment is crucial. Use environmentally friendly items, don't litter, and practice responsible tourism by staying on approved routes in national parks and refraining from touching or feeding marine life. You can ensure that future generations can appreciate the USVI's natural beauty by being aware of your environmental effect.

Use local transportation:

Taking public transit in the USVI is one of the greatest ways to explore it. There are plenty of taxis, buses, and ferries on the islands. It can be economical and convenient to go by bus or cab, and it's a terrific opportunity to meet locals and discover the island. Additionally, using ferries is a fantastic way to tour nearby islands like St. John and St. Croix.

Stay hydrated:

It's crucial to drink enough of water the entire time you're traveling because of the heat and humidity of the USVI. Drink plenty of water all day long, especially if you intend to spend time in the sun. Additionally, you might try coconut water, a famous local beverage that is hydrating and refreshing.

Plan ahead:

There is a lot to see and do in the US Virgin Islands despite its tiny size. Prioritize your activities and establish a strategy in advance to make the most of your trip. Take into account what you want to see and do, and book any tours or activities in advance. By doing this, you may avoid long queues and make the most of your stay in the USVI.

Embrace island time:

Not least, it's critical to appreciate the relaxed island lifestyle found in the USVI. It's okay if things move more slowly than you're used to. Breathe deeply, unwind, and savor the view. Allow yourself to take it easy and savor the USVI's unspoiled landscape and welcoming locals. After all, life on an island is all about that!

Chapter 1: St. Croix

The largest of the US Virgin Islands, St. Croix is situated in the Caribbean Sea and has African, European, and Caribbean influences. People of African, European, and Native American origin, as well as expatriates from all over the world, make up the island's diversified population.

Travelers seeking a balance of leisure, adventure, and cultural encounters should consider St. Croix. We would learn more about St. Croix and the benefits of going there in this chapter. St. Croix has activities to suit every taste, whether you want to see historical monuments, sample local cuisine, or just relax on a quiet beach.

Overview of the island's geography and history

The largest US Virgin Island is St. Croix, which has a total size of about 82 square miles (213 square kilometers). Approximately 40 miles (64 kilometers) south of St. Thomas and 100 miles (161 kilometers) east of Puerto Rico, the island is situated in the eastern Caribbean Sea. With its undulating hills, lush rainforests, and white sand beaches, St. Croix boasts a diverse landscape.

Native Americans, European colonists, African slaves, and more recent waves of immigrants have all had an impact on the island's rich and varied history. The Arawak and Carib peoples were St. Croix's first occupants, and they had been there for thousands of years prior to the entrance of European explorers in the 15th century.

St. Croix and numerous other islands were claimed by Spain after Christopher Columbus' Caribbean voyage in 1493. Before the Dutch arrived in the 17th century, the island was entirely deserted and underdeveloped. On St. Croix, the Dutch founded a small colony that was quickly taken over by the French, who built a sizable sugar plantation economy using slave labor from Africa.

A group of African slaves instigated a revolt against the proprietors of the estates in 1733, which resulted in the burning of numerous sugar plantations and the deaths of hundreds of people. The French and Danish authorities, who at the time shared authority of the island, put an end to the insurrection after it had lasted for several months. The Crucian Christmas Festival, which commemorates the revolt each year, is an important part of St. Croix history and culture.

When the Danish fully took over St. Croix in the late 18th century, they proceeded to expand the sugar industry, which remained the island's principal source of income until the early 20th century. St. Croix rose to prominence as a tourist destination following the collapse of the sugar industry thanks to its stunning natural surroundings, intriguing history, and lively local culture. Today, tourism dominates the island's economy as tourists from across the globe flock there to take advantage of the island's beaches, aquatic activities, and cultural attractions.

Brief introduction to the culture and people of St. Croix

Because of its past as a former Danish colony and its proximity to other Caribbean islands, St. Croix is a melting pot of cultures. People of African, European, and Hispanic heritage are among the island's diverse population. The music, artwork, and food of the island all represent this fusion of civilizations.

The island of St. Croix's African ancestry, which is commemorated via music and dance, has a significant cultural effect. On the island, people enjoy listening to traditional genres like calypso, reggae, and soca as well as the distinctive scratch band music, which uses improvised percussion instruments built from recyclable materials. Live music performances are available all year long at festivals and events, as well as at neighborhood taverns and eateries.

The island's numerous cultural influences are also reflected in its gastronomic culture. Local specialties include Caribbean-style fare like jerk chicken and rice and beans, as well as seafood delicacies like conch fritters and fish tacos. The farm-to-table movement is growing on St. Croix, where a lot of restaurants use ingredients that are acquired locally to make creative and delectable dishes.

St. Croix is renowned for its art and handicrafts in addition to its music and gastronomy. Numerous skilled artists who produce works in a range of media, such as painting, sculpture, and jewelry, call the island home. The brilliant and colorful works of these regional painters can be seen by visitors who explore the island's art studios and galleries.

St. Croix is a wonderful place to visit because of its varied people and rich cultural heritage. Visitors can learn more about and develop a greater appreciation for the island's people and culture by learning about its music, cuisine, and visual arts.

Best time to visit the island and how to get there

Best Time to Visit

The high season, which runs from December to April, is when most people travel to St. Croix since the weather is at its most comfortable and dry. The best range of Fahrenheit temperatures for outdoor pursuits like hiking, snorkeling, and diving is between the mid-70s and the mid-80s. The majority of events and festivals, such as the Crucian Christmas Festival in December and the St. Croix Food & Wine Experience in April, which highlight the island's vibrant culture and culinary sector, are also held during this season.

As they are outside of the busiest travel months and provide slightly cheaper rates and less crowds, May to August and November are regarded as the shoulder seasons. With temperatures in the upper 70s to mid 80s Fahrenheit and sporadic light rain showers, the weather is still pleasant and sunny. For those who prefer a calmer and more relaxed atmosphere, it's a perfect time to come. You can also benefit from lower airline and hotel prices.

The Caribbean hurricane season runs from June to November, and St. Croix is not exempt from this. Although it's unlikely that a hurricane would hit the island during this time, it's still vital to bear this in mind when making travel plans. It is advised to purchase travel insurance, and it is crucial to be aware of the weather and any potential storm warnings.

Depending on your specific objectives and tastes, there is no one optimum time to visit St. Croix. The high season is the best time to visit if you want warm, dry weather, exciting festivals, and a lively environment. The shoulder season can be more to your taste if you like a more relaxed atmosphere and reduced prices. No matter what time of year you visit, St. Croix has a plethora of outdoor recreation, cultural experiences, and natural beauty.

How to Get There

By Air:

Here are your alternatives for traveling by flight to St. Croix.

International Flights:

The primary entry point for travelers from outside the country is St. Croix's Henry E. Rohlsen International Airport (STX). Flights from several well-known carriers, including American carriers, Delta Air Lines, United Airlines, and JetBlue Airways, go to St. Croix. There are many significant American cities with direct flights to St. Croix, including Miami, New York, Atlanta, and Charlotte. Additionally, flights are accessible from nearby Caribbean locations like San Juan, Puerto Rico, and St. Thomas, St. Kitts.

Domestic Flights:

Should you already be in the U.S. St. Croix is also accessible via domestic flights from the Virgin Islands. Daily flights between St. Thomas and St. Croix are run by Seaborne Airlines and Cape Air, and the trip takes 20 to 30 minutes. Along with other Caribbean locations, InterCaribbean Airways also offers flights between St. Croix and St. Thomas.

Flight Duration and Frequency:

Depending on your departure city and airline, the travel time to St. Croix might vary, but it often takes between 2.5 and 4 hours from major American cities. Seasonal variations in flight frequency can also occur, with more flights being made accessible from December to April, which is the busiest travel period. Checking flight schedules and making reservations early will help you secure your preferred trip dates.

By Sea:

These are your alternatives if you're traveling to St. Croix by sea.

Ferry Services:

Regular ferry service between St. Thomas and St. Croix is provided by the Virgin Islands Ferry and Transportation Services, and the trip takes around two hours. The ferry travels between St. Thomas' Red Hook Ferry Terminal and St. Croix's Gallows Bay Dock.

Tourists who want to travel to St. Croix from nearby islands like St. Thomas or St. John frequently use the ferry service. The boat offers a relaxing and picturesque trip in the Caribbean Sea, with stunning views of the archipelago of the Virgin Islands. The boat is another cost-effective choice, with round-trip tickets costing between $50 and $60 per person.

It's crucial to prepare and make reservations in advance when taking a ferry, especially during times of high travel demand. As seats might fill up fast and ferry timings can change depending on the season, it is advised to purchase your tickets as soon as possible.

Private Boat:

Renting a private boat is another alternative for getting to St. Croix via sea. For those who want the privacy and comfort of their own watercraft while exploring the island at their own speed, this is a fantastic alternative. Local businesses provide boat rental and charter services for everything from small boats to expensive yachts.

It's crucial to plan ahead and make preparations in advance when chartering a boat, especially during periods of high travel demand. Additionally, you'll need to make sure your yacht complies with all safety standards and laws and acquire the required licenses and permits.

Traveling to St. Croix by water, whether by ferry or private boat, is a wonderful way to explore the natural beauty and serenity of the Virgin Islands.

Getting Around:

The St. Croix choices are listed here.

Renting a Car:

A popular and practical way to tour St. Croix is by renting a car, especially if you want to visit several sights or beaches in one day. There are numerous automobile rental companies in the city and at the airport that provide a variety of vehicles, including compact cars and SUVs. To rent a car on St. Croix, you must have a valid driver's license and be at least 25 years old.

It's vital to keep in mind that driving on St. Croix is done on the left side of the road, which might be challenging for those who are not accustomed to it. In some places, the roads can also be winding and narrow, so it's crucial to drive safely and abide by local rules. Additionally, parking spaces in well-known tourist sites might be hard to come by, so make sure to arrive early to guarantee a spot.

Taking a Taxi:

On St. Croix, taxis are commonly available and might be a practical transportation choice, especially if you don't wish to drive. Taxi fares are regulated by the government, and you can typically locate them at hotels, the airport, and famous tourist destinations. To avoid any misunderstandings, make careful to clarify the fare with the driver before boarding the cab.

Although they can be useful, cabs can sometimes be costly, especially if you are traveling far or in a group. It's also crucial to remember that taxi drivers might not be able to offer much commentary or knowledge about the island, so if you're eager to learn more about St. Croix, you might want to think about going on a guided tour.

Taking a Public Bus:

A public bus, commonly referred to as a "safari" bus, is a convenient and authentic way to travel throughout St. Croix. These open-air buses run on many routes all across the island and are a preferred means of transportation for both locals and visitors.

Although prices are normally low, timetables might be unpredictable and occasionally aren't advertised in advance. Typically, you can flag down a safari bus on the side of the road, but be ready to share the vehicle with other people and possibly stand for the entirety of the journey. Safari buses are an excellent way to experience the island from the perspective of the locals, but they might not be the ideal choice if you're pressed for time or have certain places in mind.

Top Attractions and Activities

Christiansted National Historic Site: Christiansted National Historic Site is a must-see destination for history and architecture buffs. With its cobblestone streets, vibrant houses, and historical sites, Christiansted serves as a charming reflection of St. Croix's colonial past. The colonial architecture of the town has been beautifully conserved, and many of the structures date to the 18th century. One of the most notable features of the location is the Fort Christiansvaern, which is regarded as one of the outstanding examples of Danish military construction in the Caribbean. The different exhibits at the fort allow visitors to discover the history of the island's colonial past. Visitors can take guided tours of the historic site, which provide an in-depth look at the history of the town.

Buck Island Reef National Monument: The Buck Island Reef National Monument is a protected marine sanctuary and one of St. Croix's busiest tourist destinations. The island's coral reefs, underground caverns, and aquatic life may all be explored by boat tours that visitors can take. Buck Island's surrounding waters are exceptionally clear and provide fantastic diving and snorkeling visibility. Diverse tropical fish, sea turtles, and other marine life are visible to visitors. The island also has a lovely beach where guests may unwind and take in the breathtaking views of the Caribbean Sea.

Estate Whim Plantation Museum: This museum offers a fascinating look at St. Croix's colonial past as a significant sugar-producing island. Estate Whim Plantation Museum. The estate, which has now been repaired and transformed into a museum, was once among the island's greatest sugar estates. Visitors can take a tour of the main home, which is furnished with antiques and historical items, and discover more about the enslaved people who lived and worked there. The museum provides a plethora of knowledge regarding the island's cultural legacy, including St. Croix's music, dance, and cuisine.

Cruzan Rum Distillery: The Cruzan Rum Distillery is one of the island's most well-liked attractions and is part of St. Croix's long-standing legacy of rum production. On a tour of the distillery, guests may learn how rum is produced, from fermentation to aging. A variety of rums, including those that are only found on the island, are tasted during the tour. Additionally, there is a gift shop where guests can buy bottles of rum to take home as mementos. In addition to tasting some of the best rum in the Caribbean, the distillery is an excellent site to learn about the history and cultural legacy of the island.

Sandy Point National Wildlife Refuge: Sandy Point National Wildlife Refuge is an undiscovered treasure for nature enthusiasts. It is a lonely beach on the southwest corner of St. Croix. The area is a designated nature reserve, and the beach is where endangered sea turtles lay their eggs. Hiking along the sandy beach offers a chance to see the local wildlife and take in the breathtaking views of the Caribbean Sea. During turtle nesting season, the beach is closed, but tourists can still explore the neighborhood and trek along the paths. The refuge is a wonderful spot to unwind and get in touch with nature because it provides a quiet and seclusion from the bustle of the city.

Salt River Bay National Historical Park and Ecological Preserve: This park is a singular fusion of scenic beauty and historical significance. Salt River Bay National Historical Park and Ecological Preserve. The park is a significant natural preserve since it includes both a coral reef and a mangrove forest. The first known contact between

Christopher Columbus and the indigenous Arawak people occurred there in 1493, during the latter's second journey to the New World. Hiking routes, kayaking through the mangrove forest, and snorkeling in the pristine waters are all available to park visitors. The park also provides unique glimpses into the ecology and history of the island through its guided excursions.

Point Udall: This beautiful lookout point provides views of the Atlantic Ocean and is situated on the easternmost point of the United States. The Millennium Monument, a huge sundial that marks the beginning of each day in the United States, is visible to those who trek to the top of the hill. Time-related and environmental preservation-related quotations are written on the monument. Point Udall offers breathtaking views and is an excellent place to catch the seaside dawn or sunset.

Sandy Point Beach: One of the most stunning beaches on the island is Sandy Point Beach, a lengthy stretch of white sand. It is a nesting area for endangered sea turtles and is situated on the southwest coast of St. Croix. Visitors are encouraged to respect the turtles and stay a safe distance from them because the beach is only open during the day. There are lots of picnic tables and shade structures for tourists to utilize, and the beach is great for swimming, tanning, and snorkeling.

Divi Carina Bay Casino: Visit the Divi Carina Bay Casino for some gaming fun if you're feeling lucky. The casino offers roulette, blackjack, poker, and slot machines, and there are many chances to hit it big. Additionally, there is a sports bar and restaurant on the property where guests may get something to eat or drink while they play.

Gallows Bay: Gallows Bay is a lovely seaside neighborhood that's perfect for exploring, dining, and shopping. The neighborhood is named after the gallows that stood in this location during the colonial era and is now a hive of activity. Visitors can peruse the boutiques and shops, try regional fare at the cafes and restaurants, and take in the bustling environment. There is a marina nearby where guests can hire boats or arrange for fishing charters.

These are just a few more examples of the numerous sights and things to do in St. Croix. There is something on this lovely island for everyone, whether you like history, the outdoors, or just lounging on the beach. St. Croix is the ideal location for a tropical escape because of its warm climate, welcoming locals, and relaxed environment.

Best Beaches

Sandy Point Beach is a must-see for anybody visiting the island because it is one of St. Croix's most well-known beaches. The beach, which lies near the southernmost point of the island, is a portion of the Sandy Point National Wildlife Refuge, so it is only accessible on weekends from April to August, when turtles are laying their eggs there. Although visitors are welcome to stroll along the beach, they must not annoy the turtles that are nesting or their eggs.

The beach is a particularly lovely spot to come during turtle nesting season. One of the most amazing natural phenomena in the world can be seen if you're fortunate enough to be around when the turtles are hatching. The beach is also renowned for its pristine seas and snow-white sand, which make it the perfect location for swimming and tanning.

Cane Bay Beach: A short drive from Frederiksted, Cane Bay Beach is situated on the north side of St. Croix. The beach is a well-liked location for snorkeling and diving due to its gorgeous coral reefs and vibrant marine life. The well-known "Wall," a steep underwater drop-off that draws expert divers from all over the world, is another feature of the beach.

Snorkeling allows non-divers to take in the beauty of the underwater environment. There are many facilities at the beach, such as restrooms, showers, and a beach bar. You can rent kayaks or paddleboards and explore the neighboring coves and bays if you're up for an adventure.

Rainbow Beach: A short drive from Frederiksted, Rainbow Beach is situated on St. Croix's west coast. The beach boasts several facilities, including restrooms, showers, a beach bar and restaurant, and calm seas that are ideal for swimming. Both locals and visitors enjoy the beach, and there is always a lively and enjoyable environment there.

The rainbow-colored sand that lines the shore is one of Rainbow Beach's most distinctive characteristics. Due to the presence of minerals like garnet and olivine, the sand is colored, giving the beach a wonderfully spectacular aspect. Water sports like windsurfing and kayaking are also very popular at the beach, and tourists may rent the necessary gear there.

A short distance from the town of Frederiksted, Frederiksted Beach is situated on the west coast of St. Croix. The beach offers breathtaking Caribbean Sea sunsets, and the calm, shallow water makes it the perfect place for swimming and tanning. There are many facilities along the beach, including bathrooms, showers, a beach bar, and a restaurant.

The old pier that protrudes into the water is one of Frederiksted Beach's most distinctive characteristics. The pier, which is today a well-liked location for fishing and strolling, was constructed in the early 1900s to accommodate ships delivering sugar cane to the island. Water sports like paddleboarding and kayaking are also very popular at the beach, and tourists may rent the necessary gear from the surrounding vendors.

Overall, St. Croix's beaches have something to offer everyone, from quiet, beautiful stretches of sand to lively, celebratory locations with lots of services. The beaches in St. Croix won't let you down whether you're seeking for a peaceful retreat or an exciting new location to discover.

Dining and Nightlife

St. Croix has a wide range of dining establishments, from chic fine-dining establishments to laid-back coastal eateries. Some of the island's specialties include farm-to-table food, seafood, and local Caribbean cuisine.

Dining:

Savant: For foodies visiting St. Croix, Savant is a must-try restaurant. The restaurant's cozy garden atmosphere is ideal for a special event or a romantic evening. With meals like seared scallops with mango chutney, pan-roasted duck breast with ginger and plum sauce, and Thai green curry with prawns, the menu combines Caribbean, European, and Asian flavors. There are also vegetarian and vegan options, like roasted eggplant with tahini and chickpea curry. The wine list at Savant is expertly chosen and features both foreign and domestic wines. Soft lighting, candles, and live music are used to enhance the restaurant's romantic environment on specific evenings.

Rowdy Joe's: Both locals and visitors enjoy hanging out at Rowdy Joe's. After a day of seeing the island, it is the ideal place to unwind due to its beachfront setting and laid-back atmosphere. Conch fritters, jerk chicken, and lobster mac & cheese are just a few of the foods on the menu that combine American and Caribbean cuisines. A variety of tropical cocktails, regional beers, and frozen drinks are also available at the restaurant. Take advantage of the daily happy hour deals and weekend live music.

Kendrick's: Located at The Buccaneer resort, Kendrick's is a classy fine-dining restaurant. The restaurant has a view of the ocean and offers breathtaking sunsets. When possible, products from local sources are used to produce modern Caribbean food. Outstanding menu items include grilled filet mignon with truffle mashed potatoes, pan-seared fish with coconut risotto, and lobster bisque with cognac. There is a wide variety of great wines from all around the world on the large wine list. The setting and service at Kendrick's are ideal for a special occasion or a romantic supper.

Cafe Christine: In a historic building in Christiansted, there is a small café called Cafe Christine. The menu, which is French-inspired, is often updated and is made using seasonal, fresh ingredients. Escargots in garlic butter, coq au vin with red wine sauce, and seafood bouillabaisse are a few of the meals to try. A wide range of desserts, including fresh sorbet and ice cream, are produced by the pastry chef. French and foreign wines are featured on the well crafted wine list of Cafe Christine. It's the ideal location for a romantic evening or a private supper with friends because of the cozy atmosphere, which includes lighted tables and soft music.

From laid-back coastal cafes to sophisticated fine-dining establishments, St. Croix provides a wide variety of dining alternatives. There is something for every taste and budget among the island's assortment of international and indigenous delicacies available to visitors.

Nightlife:

Rhythms at Rainbow Beach:

One of the most popular places for nightlife in St. Croix is Rhythms at Rainbow Beach. This beach club, which is noted for its lively ambiance and live music, is situated directly on Frederiksted's stunning Rainbow Beach. The bar offers a selection of tropical cocktails and regional beers, and local artists frequently perform reggae and Caribbean-inspired music there. Anyone searching for a spectacular night out should definitely stop by Rhythms at Rainbow Beach with its open-air setting and stunning views of the Caribbean Sea.

Duggan's Reef:

In the East End of St. Croix, Duggan's Reef is a beachside pub and restaurant renowned for its laid-back vibe and breathtaking ocean views. The establishment serves a selection of tropical beverages and regional ales and frequently hosts live music on the weekends. Visitors at Duggan's Reef can eat or drink while admiring the mesmerizing vistas of the Caribbean's blue waters. The bar is especially well-liked during sunset, when guests may enjoy the breathtaking sunset over the ocean.

40 Strand Eatery:

40 Strand Eatery is a well-known restaurant and pub that provides a distinctive nightlife experience, and it is situated in the center of Christiansted. The bar offers a selection of craft beers and cocktails, as well as a menu of small nibbles. Drinks and meals can be enjoyed inside the trendy and stylish bar or outside on the patio that looks out over the old town. Due to its inventive cocktails and fun atmosphere, the bar enjoys a high level of popularity both among locals and tourists.

The Pickled Greek:

Christiansted is home to the well-liked tavern and eatery known as The Pickled Greek, which is renowned for its laid-back atmosphere and food with a Mediterranean influence. There is live music on the weekends at the bar, along with a selection of artisan beers and beverages. Drinks and meals can be enjoyed within the bar's warm and relaxed atmosphere or outside on the patio that looks out over the city's historic downtown. The bar is especially well-liked for its cozy and welcoming ambiance and its variety of delectable and distinctive beverages.

There are numerous nightlife alternatives available to St. Croix visitors, with something to fit every taste and price range. St. Croix offers both busy beach bars and stylish city lounges, depending on your preferences. St. Croix is one of the best places in the Caribbean for nightlife, and it's no surprise given the island's pleasant climate, gorgeous scenery, and hospitable population.

Other popular places for nightlife in St. Croix include:

The Bombay Club: The Bombay Club is a posh bar and lounge that is situated in Christiansted. The bar serves a wide variety of elegant wines and spirits, as well as classic and innovative cocktails. It's a wonderful location for a romantic evening out or a special occasion because of the sophisticated and stylish ambience.

Cheeseburgers in Paradise: In the village of Christiansted, there is a well-known beachfront restaurant and pub called Cheeseburgers in Paradise. The pub serves tasty burgers and other American-style food in addition to a selection of tropical cocktails and regional beers. Visitors can savor their meals and beverages while seeing the breathtaking Caribbean Sea.

The Blue Moon Bar & Grill: The Blue Moon Bar & Grill is a well-known nightlife destination in Frederiksted. There is frequently live music on the weekends in the bar, which serves a variety of tropical cocktails and regional beers. The bar's outside setting, which views out over the stunning Frederiksted Beach, is where patrons may enjoy their beverages and meals.

Beach Side Cafe: In Frederiksted, there is a relaxed beach pub called the Beach Side Cafe. Along with a choice of light food and drinks, the bar also serves local beers and tropical drinks. While relaxing on the beach and taking in the stunning views of the Caribbean Sea, visitors can savor their beverages and meals.

No matter what kind of nightlife you choose, St. Croix has a wide range of interesting pubs, lounges, and dining options. St. Croix offers something for everyone, whether you want to have a romantic evening with your significant other, dance the night away to live music, or simply relax with a chilled drink after a day of touring the island.

Where to Stay

A variety of lodging options are available in St. Croix, from opulent beachfront resorts to comfortable boutique hotels and guesthouses. Everyone can find something on this island, whether they're seeking for a budget-friendly getaway, a family-friendly resort, or a romance getaway.

The Buccaneer:

The Buccaneer is a wonderfully opulent resort that has been run by families for many years. It is simple to understand why it is one of the most renowned and historic properties on the island of St. Croix. The 340 acres of lush tropical plants around the resort create a tranquil and relaxing ambiance for visitors to enjoy.

Each of the 138 nicely furnished guestrooms and suites at the resort has a private balcony or patio with views of the golf course or the sea. The accommodations offer all the contemporary comforts and conveniences that guests would require for a comfortable stay in rooms that are roomy, cozy, and nicely designed.

The three private beaches at The Buccaneer, which are only accessible to resort visitors, are one of its features. These beaches are undeveloped and quiet, making them the ideal location for unwinding and enjoying the Caribbean sun. The resort also has one of the top 18-hole golf courses in the Caribbean. Golfers will adore the difficult layout and the breathtaking ocean views that can be seen from several of the holes.

The Buccaneer includes a full-service spa that provides a variety of treatments and services for visitors who want to unwind and revitalize. Visitors can indulge in a variety of spa services, including as massages, facials, and body wraps, that will leave them feeling revitalized and invigorated.

Food lovers will also enjoy The Buccaneer's dining selections. Four restaurants and bars are available in the resort, each with a distinctive menu and setting. Every taste and occasion may be satisfied, from elegant dining to relaxed seaside food.

The Buccaneer provides visitors with a variety of water sports and activities in addition to all of these amenities. There are numerous activities accessible, like snorkeling, kayaking, paddleboarding, and sailing, so visitors won't be bored while there.

In conclusion, The Buccaneer is the ideal option for couples, families, and golf fans looking for a chic and tranquil holiday. This resort offers everything visitors could want for an amazing getaway, including opulent lodgings, breathtaking beaches, a top-notch golf course, a full-service spa, and delectable dining options.

Sand Castle on the Beach:

On the west coast of the island near Frederiksted, there is a quaint and cozy boutique hotel called Sand Castle on the Beach. For those looking for a peaceful and romantic holiday, this charming hotel offers a distinctive and genuine Caribbean experience. The hotel is next to a quiet beach where visitors may take advantage of the Caribbean Sea's beautiful turquoise waves and golden dunes.

The 25 individually furnished rooms and suites at Sand Castle on the Beach are one of the hotel's features. All rooms have modern facilities including air conditioning, cable TV, Wi-Fi, and private balconies or patios overlooking the sea or the tropical gardens, each with its own Caribbean-inspired theme and design, such as the "Mermaid's Lair" or the "Hibiscus Suite."

Sand Castle on the Beach's magnificent tropical gardens give visitors a tranquil and loving ambiance. The hotel has a lovely pool, hot tub, and hammocks, making it the ideal place for visitors to relax and take in the Caribbean sun. Couples and honeymooners will find the hotel to be the perfect choice due to its serene and pleasant atmosphere.

Both visitors and locals enjoy eating at the on-site restaurant, Beach Side Cafe. Using only the freshest ingredients and spices, the restaurant delivers Caribbean cuisine and fresh local seafood. Meals can be had in front of the hotel's lush tropical gardens or the breathtaking Caribbean Sea.

Additionally, Sand Castle on the Beach is ideally situated close to a number of activities and sights. Visitors can join a scuba diving adventure to see the island's underwater wonders, tour the St. Croix Coral Reef National Monument, or stroll around Frederiksted's historic center.

For those looking for a peaceful and romantic escape, Sand Castle on the Beach provides a distinctive and genuine Caribbean experience. Couples, honeymooners, and tourists looking for a tranquil and genuine Caribbean experience will adore this delightful hotel's exquisite rooms and suites, lush tropical gardens, and great on-site dining options.

Caravelle Hotel and Casino:

One of the most affordable hotels in St. Croix is the Caravelle Hotel and Casino. It provides a strategic location in Christiansted, the island's largest town, and serves as a fantastic starting point for exploring the neighborhood. The historic Fort Christiansvaern and the Christiansted Boardwalk, which is dotted with stores, eateries, and bars, are just a short stroll from the hotel.

There are 43 inviting guestrooms and suites available at the hotel, all of which feature air conditioning, flat-screen TVs, mini-fridges, and complimentary Wi-Fi. Many of the rooms have stunning views of the port or the ocean and are roomy and well-appointed. Depending on their requirements and interests, guests can select from a variety of room categories, including ordinary rooms, deluxe rooms, and suites.

The Caravelle's rooftop pool, lounge, and bar, which offers breathtaking panoramic views of the Christiansted shoreline and the surrounding hills, is one of its best features. Visitors can unwind on the lounge chairs, dip in the hot tub, or sip a cool beverage at the bar while admiring the scenery. The rooftop is a terrific place to take in the Caribbean breeze or the sunset.

The Caravelle's on-site casino, which provides a variety of gambling options such slot machines, table games, and sports betting, is another distinctive aspect of the hotel. The casino is a well-liked destination for locals and visitors looking to try their luck and have fun because it is open around-the-clock.

A number of dining alternatives are also available at the hotel, including Caravelle Market, which sells sandwiches, fresh coffee, croissants, and pastries, and RumRunners Restaurant, which serves a selection of Caribbean and international cuisine. Visitors can also check out the close-by pubs and eateries on the Christiansted Boardwalk, which have a variety of fare and settings.

In conclusion, the Caravelle Hotel and Casino is a fantastic choice for tourists on a tight budget who want to be close to the action and enjoy a pleasant and relaxed atmosphere. The Caravelle is a well-liked alternative for travelers to St. Croix thanks to its convenient location, pleasant accommodations, rooftop pool and bar, on-site casino, and culinary options.

The Palms at Pelican Cove:

The Palms at Pelican Cove is a very exceptional resort that provides honeymooners and couples with a one-of-a-kind and unforgettable experience. This boutique beachside resort, which is a hidden gem, is situated on the island's north shore in the Christiansted neighborhood of La Grande

Princesse. It offers a peaceful and romantic escape from the bustle of daily life.

The resort has 40 roomy, elegant suites, each with a separate patio or balcony overlooking the water. Each suite is thoughtfully furnished with soft bedding, stylish decor, and contemporary conveniences like air conditioning, flat-screen TVs, and Wi-Fi in mind for your pleasure and enjoyment. Additionally, the rooms come with kitchenettes or full kitchens, making it simple to make meals and snacks whenever you want.

The resort's private beach, which provides a beautiful and seclusion location for sunbathing, swimming, and snorkeling, is without a doubt its best feature. It's the ideal setting for romantic strolls or just relaxing in a hammock with a good book because the beach is surrounded by beautiful tropical gardens and palm trees.

The resort has a swimming pool and hot tub in addition to the beach, both of which give breathtaking views of the water and offer a cool respite from the Caribbean sun. There are cozy loungers and umbrellas surrounding the pool area, as well as a poolside bar where you may sip a cool cocktail or eat a little snack.

The resort's on-site restaurant, The Palms Restaurant, serves fresh regional seafood and other cuisines from across the world. With options for both indoor and outdoor sitting, the restaurant lets you enjoy your meal while taking in the scenery of the ocean or tropical plants. Along with a variety of premium wines and beverages, the restaurant also hosts live music on some evenings.

The Palms at Pelican Cove offers a variety of excursions and activities, including as snorkeling, diving, fishing, and island tours, for people who want to explore the island. The kind and educated staff at the resort can assist you with itinerary planning and reservations for nearby attractions.

The Palms at Pelican Cove is a great option for honeymooners and couples looking to get away to a quiet, romantic location. This resort is undoubtedly a hidden treasure on the island of St. Croix because to its breathtaking beachfront setting, chic and comfortable lodgings, and first-rate restaurants and amenities.

In conclusion, St. Croix offers a wide range of accommodations to meet your interests and needs, whether you're seeking for an opulent resort, a quiet boutique hotel, or a reasonably priced option. Make sure to reserve your lodging in advance.

Chapter 2: St. John

Introduction to St. John

St. John is a tiny, picture-perfect island in the US Virgin Islands that is well-known for its gorgeous beaches, clean waters, and lush tropical vegetation. There are about 5,000 people living on the island, which is only four miles broad and nine miles long.

The Arawak and Carib tribes, who lived on the island before European colonization, had a significant impact on the history of St. John. The United States purchased the island in 1917 to be included in the US Virgin Islands after it was eventually claimed by Denmark in the 17th century.

Today, eco-tourism initiatives and St. John's breathtaking natural beauty are the city's main draws. Two-thirds of the island is covered by the Virgin Islands National Park, which provides numerous options for outdoor recreation along with hiking trails, beaches, and coral reefs.

With its steep hills, rugged cliffs, and lush valleys, St. John's topography offers stunning views of the Caribbean Sea from almost every direction. St. John has a tropical climate with year-round average temperatures in the mid-70s to mid-80s Fahrenheit.

Visitors to St. John can travel there by air through the Cyril E. King Airport on St. Thomas or by ferry from the nearby island of St. Thomas. Visitors can enjoy the island's breathtaking beaches, natural wonders, and lively local culture once they arrive.

Overall, St. John is a destination that nature lovers and outdoor enthusiasts must visit since it offers a distinctive fusion of unspoiled natural beauty, extensive history, and lively local culture.

History and culture of St. John

The history and culture of St. John go back to pre-Columbian times. The Taino people, who were expert farmers and fisherman, lived on the island. After the Spanish arrived in the late 15th century, the Taino population started to dwindle, and in the 17th century, the Danish West India Company began to seize the island.

When the corporation established a sugar plantation on the island in 1718, the Danish colonization of St. John officially began. Africans who had been sold into slavery were brought to the island to labor on the sugar cane plantations, which eventually became St. John's main source of income. The Danish West Indies were sold to the United States in 1917, and slavery was banned on the island in 1848.

Today, the Virgin Islands National Park, which has a number of historical sites and landmarks, preserves St. John's past. One of the most well-liked sights provides a look into the island's colonial past and the legacy of slavery at the Annaberg Sugar Plantation. The plantation's remains are open for visitors to explore, where they can discover how sugar is made.

St. John has a rich cultural heritage that draws on the island's distinctive fusion of African, European, and Caribbean influences. Rastafarians, Christians, and other religious and spiritual groups are among the island's diverse population of locals and visitors.

Music, artwork, and cuisine are used to celebrate the cultural legacy of St. John. Calypso, reggae, and steel pan music are just a few of the local celebrations and events that highlight the island's musical and dancing traditions, like Carnival and the St. John Festival. African, European, and Caribbean flavors are combined with seafood, tropical fruits, and spices to create the island's cuisine.

St. John's culture is also influenced by its surroundings, with a focus on sustainability and environmental protection. The ecotourism sector of the island encourages outdoor pursuits including hiking, snorkeling, and kayaking with an emphasis on eco-friendly travel methods and minimizing environmental damage.

Overall, St. John's history and culture offer a fascinating backdrop against which travelers can discover and take in the island's natural beauty and different populations.

Overview of the island's geography and climate

The US Virgin Islands' St. John is a tiny island that is only 20 square miles in size. The island is located in the Caribbean Sea just south of the British Virgin Islands and east of Puerto Rico. Because so much of the island is protected by the Virgin Islands National Park, St. John is renowned for its natural beauty.

The island's landscape is made up of rocky beaches, steep hills, and dense tropical woods. Bordeaux Mountain, which is 1,277 feet tall, is the island's highest point. It can be difficult for drivers who are not accustomed to steep inclines and abrupt curves to navigate the island's network of narrow roads that connect its numerous hills and valleys.

The climate in St. John's is tropical, with mild temperatures and high humidity all year long. Due to its location in the path of the trade winds, the island benefits from frequent cooling breezes. On average, the island experiences temperatures between the mid-70s and the mid-80s Fahrenheit, including brief heat waves during the summer. On St. John, the rainy season lasts from May to November, with September and October often seeing the biggest downpours. Visitors should be ready for sporadic thunderstorms and torrential downpours throughout this period.

A wide variety of plants and wildlife may thrive on the island due to its tropical temperature and lush vegetation. More than 800 different types of plants and trees can be found in the Virgin Islands National Park, including imposing mahogany trees, aromatic frangipani, and delicate orchids. Many different species of colorful fish, sea turtles, and other marine life may be found in the coral reefs on the island. Hiking, snorkeling, and kayaking are just a few of the outdoor activities available to St. John visitors as they enjoy the island's natural splendor.

Overall, St. John is a unique and fascinating destination for tourists seeking to take in the natural beauty of the Caribbean thanks to its geography and climate. St. John is certain to create a lasting impression, whether you're exploring the island's tropical forests, unwinding on its white sand beaches, or taking in the local cuisine and culture.

Getting to St. John (ferry and air travel)

Even though St. John is the smallest of the three islands that make up the US Virgin Islands, it is nevertheless a very well-liked tourism destination. Fortunately, there are several options available for travelers to choose from when trying to reach St. John.

Ferry Travel:
Taking a ferry from either St. Thomas or the British Virgin Islands is one of the most well-liked ways to get to St. John. There are numerous ferry companies that run services between St. Thomas and St. John, and the ferry terminal in St. Thomas is situated in Red Hook. The Caribbean Sea and other islands are spectacularly visible from the ship during the 20–30 minute trip.

Taking a ferry from the British Virgin Islands to St. John is an additional choice. The British Virgin Islands and St. John are connected by ferries run by Native Son Ferry, Speedy's, and Inter-Island Boat Services. It's crucial to remember that there are a few immigration and customs rules that must be adhered to when traveling between the US and the British Virgin Islands.

Air Travel:
There isn't an airport on St. John, but travelers can fly into St. Thomas' Cyril E. King Airport, which is about 20 miles away. Visitors can then take a taxi or a rental car to the Red Hook ferry station where they can catch a ferry to St. John. An alternative is to book a private water taxi or charter boat to take travelers directly to St. John from the airport.

It's important to keep in mind that flights to St. Thomas can be costly and challenging to find during the busiest travel period (usually November through April). Visitors should also be mindful of the Cyril E. King Airport's minimal amenities and potential for lengthy queues at immigration and customs.

Visitors should make travel arrangements in advance and be aware of any travel restrictions or laws that might be in force as a result of the continuing COVID-19 outbreak. If there are any updates or changes to the travel policies, it's vital to verify with the local authorities as well as the airline or boat company.

Visitors should also be aware that ferry schedules might change depending on the time of year and the day of the week. It is always a good idea to check the schedule in advance to avoid any unforeseen delays or cancellations.

It is advised to reserve flights as early as possible for those traveling by air to ensure the greatest prices and availability. The length of the customs and immigration processes, which can range from 30 minutes to several hours depending on the volume of travelers and the time of day, should also be taken into consideration by visitors.

Visitors can use the island's public transit, a taxi, or a rental car once they arrive on St. John to travel around. Due to the tiny and twisting roads, driving might be difficult, thus it is advised to use caution and abide by local traffic laws.

The voyage to St. John, whether by air or ferry, is reasonably simple, and the island's breathtaking natural beauty and laid-back atmosphere make the trip well worth it. Just remember to make a schedule, adhere to any rules of the road, and have fun!

Top Attractions and Activities

Visit the Virgin Islands National Park, covering two-thirds of the island:
The Virgin Islands National Park, which occupies more than two-thirds of the island, is located on St. John. Beautiful

beaches, luxuriant woods, and vivid coral reefs are just a few of the park's many natural wonders. The park has a variety of hiking paths that guests can enjoy, from short strolls to strenuous excursions across rocky terrain. The Reef Bay Trail, which leads to a historic sugar plantation and petroglyphs created by the island's native people, and the Cinnamon Bay Trail, which provides breathtaking views of the island's north shore, are two of the most well-known paths.

Explore the coral reefs surrounding St. John:

St. John is a great place to go snorkeling and scuba diving because of the clean waters and vibrant coral reefs that surround it. To view vibrant fish, sea turtles, and other marine life, tourists can either hire equipment or go on a guided tour to explore the underwater environment. Some of the greatest locations for snorkeling and diving are Hawksnest Bay, which has a variety of coral formations, and Trunk Bay, which has an underwater snorkeling route.

Take a boat tour to the nearby British Virgin Islands:

The British Virgin Islands, which are close to St. John and have their own special attractions and experiences, are nearby. The islands can be explored on a boat tour that makes pit stops at charming beaches, snorkeling locations, and native settlements. Popular vacation spots include Virgin Gorda, which has the renowned Baths rock formations and isolated bays, and Jost Van Dyke, which is well-known for its energetic beach bars and reggae music.

Learn about the island's history at the Annaberg Sugar Plantation:

Before European colonization, the Taino native people inhabited the island for thousands of years, leaving behind a rich history for St. John. The Annaberg Sugar Plantation, which ran from the 18th to the 19th century and was a notable producer of sugar and molasses, is one of the most important historical sites on St. John. In addition to learning about the lives of the enslaved Africans who worked there and the intricate social and economic institutions that formed life on the island, visitors can enjoy a guided walk of the plantation ruins.

Discover the island's art and culture:
A thriving arts scene can be found in St. John, where there are numerous studios and galleries that feature the work of regional artists. In addition to the surrounding Coral Bay Village, famed for its bohemian vibe and unique mix of stores and restaurants, visitors can explore the Mongoose Junction shopping complex, which houses a variety of boutiques, cafés, and art galleries. The island also organizes other cultural occasions all year long, such as the July St. John Festival, which includes parades, music, and food.

Experience the island's beaches:
The beautiful beaches of St. John are well known for their white sand, crystal-clear water, and spectacular scenery. On the island, there are more than 30 beaches to explore, each with its own special charm and personality. Trunk Bay, Cinnamon Bay, and Maho Bay are among of the busiest beaches and provide a variety of facilities and activities, such as kayaking, snorkeling, and beachside dining.

Try the local cuisine:
A variety of eateries and food trucks providing Caribbean and foreign cuisine can be found throughout St. John. Conch fritters, jerk chicken, shellfish, and other regional specialties are available for tourists to sample, in addition to worldwide cuisine with a local touch. A variety of cocktails, beers, and wines are available at the island's vibrant bar scene, which

includes beachside bars, rooftop lounges, and live music venues.

Relax and unwind:
 As a result of its well-known easygoing atmosphere, St. John is a great place to unwind and get away from the pressures of daily life. Visitors can indulge in spa services, yoga sessions, and wellness pursuits or just unwind on the beach and enjoy the sunshine. St. John offers an island retreat that is genuinely unforgettably beautiful because to its abundant natural beauty, rich culture, and friendly society.

St. John has a wide variety of sights to see and things to do that highlight the island's stunning natural surroundings, fascinating history, and lively culture. Everyone can find something to do in St. John, whether they want to take a trek through the jungle, unwind on the beach, or discover the underwater world.

Top Beaches

Trunk Bay
 One of the most well-known beaches on the island is Trunk Bay, which is situated on the north side of St. John. It is renowned for its immaculate white sand beach and turquoise sea. The beach is flanked by palm palms and verdant hills, making it a beautiful backdrop for swimming and tanning. Trunk Bay's underwater snorkeling route, which offers tourists an educational tour of the coral reef and the marine species that calls it home, is one of its distinctive attractions. Underwater markers that indicate various fish, coral, and other marine life species line the trail. In addition, Trunk Bay has amenities like a snack bar, showers, and restrooms.

Cinnamon Bay
 Families and lovers of water sports flock to Cinnamon Bay, which is on St. John's north shore. The beach is an excellent place for swimming, kayaking, and stand-up paddleboarding because of the calm waves and broad expanse of white sand.

A camping area and a number of hiking routes, including one that goes to the ruins of an old sugar mill nearby, are also located in Cinnamon Bay. There are facilities like bathrooms, showers, and picnic tables at the beach.

Maho Bay
Maho Bay is a quiet beach with calm, shallow water that is situated on the north side of St. John. The beach is a well-liked location for relaxing and snorkeling because of its serene ambiance and stunning surroundings. Many people have mentioned seeing sea turtles swimming around Maho Bay, which is well-known for regular sightings of these friendly animals. The beach has facilities like restrooms, showers, and a snack bar and is flanked by hills that are lush and green.

These three beaches serve as some of the best representations of the island's breathtaking natural beauty. St. John is well known for its beautiful beaches. Make it a point to visit these beaches while in St. John and partake in the water sports, snorkeling, and other things they have to offer.

Dining and Nightlife

The Beach Bar:
The Beach Bar, which is situated on the Cruz Bay shoreline, is a favorite hangout for both tourists and residents. The Beach Bar is a terrific spot to unwind and enjoy a tasty meal or a tropical cocktail thanks to its lively environment, beachside setting, and live music. Conch fritters, fish tacos, and jerk chicken are just a few of the Caribbean-inspired items on the menu. There are also traditional American cuisine like burgers and salads. The bar also serves a selection of beer, wine, and cocktails.

The Longboard:
The Longboard is a relaxed dining establishment with a focus on American and Caribbean food that is situated in Cruz Bay. The menu offers items crafted with fresh, regional ingredients, like poke bowls, fish tacos, burgers, and salads. Outdoor seating, a bright interior, and a laid-back, surf-inspired ambiance define the restaurant. In addition, The Longboard is renowned for its wide variety of specialty beers and inventive cocktails.

The Tap Room at Mongoose Junction:
The Tap Room, a favorite hangout for beer enthusiasts, is situated in Cruz Bay's Mongoose Junction shopping mall. The pub offers a choice of bottled beers and ciders in addition to a constantly changing tap list of regional and worldwide craft brews. Additionally, there are pub classics like burgers, wings, and nachos on the menu. There are indoor and outdoor seating options in the comfortable, rustic setting of The Tap Room.

The Lime Inn:
Since 1984, the family-run The Lime Inn restaurant in Cruz Bay has been offering food with a Caribbean influence. Fresh seafood, grilled meats, and vegetarian selections are all available on the menu and are all created with locally sourced ingredients. The restaurant also features a sizable wine selection and a full bar. The Lime Inn is a favorite among both locals and tourists because of its lovely, laid-back ambiance.

High Tide Bar and Seafood Grill:
Cruz Bay's High Tide is a beachside eatery and bar with a breathtaking view of the port. Fresh seafood, sushi, and other Caribbean-inspired foods are available on the menu, along with a variety of beverages and wines. On certain

nights, the restaurant also features live music and a joyful, tropical ambiance.

The Terrace:
The Terrace, a gourmet dining establishment with expansive views of the sea and adjacent islands, is situated within the Caneel Bay Resort. With an emphasis on using products that are fresh and locally produced, the menu offers a blend of Caribbean and international cuisine. The restaurant is ideal for a special event or a romantic evening because of its posh, classy ambiance.

Cruz Bay Landing:
Cruz Bay Landing is a relaxed eatery and bar that serves a fusion of American and Caribbean food. Burgers, sandwiches, salads, and seafood meals are available on the menu. A complete bar with beer and tropical cocktails is also available. Additionally, there is live music occasionally and a daily happy hour at the restaurant.

To accommodate all tastes and price ranges, St. John provides a wide variety of food and nightlife options. Visitors are sure to find something that suits their preferences, from informal eateries with fresh, local cuisine to seaside pubs with live music. The bar scene on the island is also growing, with many establishments serving inventive cocktails, artisan beer, and regional rum specialties.

Where to Stay

Caneel Bay Resort:
In the Virgin Islands National Park, on a peninsula spanning 170 acres, is the opulent Caneel Bay Resort. Seven hidden beaches, each with its own distinct personality and aesthetic, can be found at the resort, which also offers facilities including guided excursions, spa services, and rentals for various water sports gear. Each of the 166 guestrooms and

suites at the resort has a private patio or balcony with views of the garden or the beach. The resort provides a variety of sports like kayaking, sailing, and snorkeling, as well as many dining options, including a beachfront restaurant.

The Westin St. John Resort Villas:
On Great Cruz Bay, there is a family-friendly resort called The Westin St. John Resort Villas. The resort has a number of pools and hot tubs, a fitness center, and a spa in addition to its own private beach. The villas come with a living room, a kitchenette or complete kitchen, a private balcony or patio, and are available in a variety of layouts, from studio to three-bedroom units. Along with a host of on-site facilities and activities, the resort also has a kids' club, tennis courts, and a number of water sports.

Private vacation rentals:
In St. John, private vacation rentals are a well-liked choice, and many villas and apartments are offered for rent through various internet booking services. These vacation rentals, which can range from modest studio flats to roomy luxury villas, provide a more private and intimate experience than standard resorts. While some accommodations provide access to local beaches or other amenities, others might have a private pool or hot tub. Private vacation rentals may not offer the same level of service and amenities as conventional resorts, and guests will need to make their own travel and activity arrangements.

St. John offers a variety of lodging alternatives, from pricey resorts to more economical vacation homes, to suit a variety of tastes and budgets. St. John has something to offer whether you're seeking for a single adventure, a family holiday, or a romantic retreat.

Before making a reservation, it is crucial to do your homework and compare the available lodging alternatives in St. John because they might range greatly in terms of cost, location, and amenities. When selecting a place to stay in St. John, keep the following extra aspects in mind:

Location: Your stay's location can significantly affect how you feel about St. John as a whole. Consider lodging in Cruz Bay, the island's major town, if you want to be close to the beach or can walk to restaurants and shopping. Look for alternatives on the more sedate parts of the island, such Coral Bay or the East End, if you prefer a more private and serene atmosphere.

Amenities: When selecting a place to stay in St. John, you may wish to give particular features priority depending on your travel tastes and style. For instance, if you intend to spend a lot of time at the beach, search for a resort or vacation home that offers beach access and equipment rentals for water activities. Consider renting a home or apartment with a private pool or hot tub if you desire privacy and seclusion.

Budget: St. John can be pricey, especially from December to April when it's busy. Guesthouses, campgrounds, and vacation rentals in less popular places are nevertheless possibilities for budget-conscious tourists. Before making a reservation, make sure to shop about and read reviews to make sure you are getting a good deal.

Sustainability: St. John is known for its eco-tourism and environmentally friendly travel methods, so think about booking a stay at a resort or vacation home that places an emphasis on environmental protection and neighborhood involvement. Choose products that utilize renewable energy, cut down on trash, and aid regional projects.

The ideal accommodation in St. John will ultimately depend on your own tastes and trip objectives. Whether you decide on an opulent resort, a homey villa, or a comfortable rental, St. John will undoubtedly provide an unforgettable and revitalizing island break.

Extra Tips

Support regional companies who have an emphasis on environmental preservation and community involvement as St. John is noted for its eco-tourism and sustainable travel practices:

The economy of St. John, a lovely but vulnerable ecology, is primarily reliant on tourism. As a result, it's critical to support companies who are dedicated to protecting the island's natural resources and encouraging ethical tourist methods. The following are some ways you can contribute:

- Pick eco-friendly lodgings that recycle garbage, use renewable energy, and consume little water.
- Select locally run companies that value neighborhood involvement and the local economy. Look for the "Made in the VI" mark or enquire about the company's sustainable policies from the owner.
- Take part in environmentally friendly activities when traveling, such as kayaking, snorkeling, and hiking.
- Assist conservation organizations that aim to save the island's wildlife and natural resources, such as the Virgin Islands National Park.

Since the island's topography can be difficult for outdoor activities and the sun can be severe, be sure to pack lots of water, sunscreen, and insect repellent:

St. John is a tropical island with a hot, muggy atmosphere that, if you're unprepared, may be hard on your body. The following points should be remembered:

- To protect your skin from the sun's damaging rays, use sunscreen with a high SPF. Apply it often, particularly if you're swimming or perspiring.
- Pack insect repellent to keep off mosquitoes and other bugs, which can be especially troublesome from May through November during the rainy season.
- Avoid sugary or alcoholic beverages, which can dehydrate you, and drink lots of water.
- Dress comfortably for outdoor activities such as hiking, swimming, and other outdoor sports.

Try to learn some basic Creole or Patois words to communicate with locals while observing local customs, notably those of the island's Christian and Rastafarian communities:

The island of St. John is cosmopolitan and diversified, and it has a long history and distinctive traditions. Here are some considerations to bear in mind in order to get the most out of your trip and prevent cultural misunderstandings:

- Dress modestly and refrain from actions that can be construed as insulting or offensive in order to show respect to the island's Christian and Rastafarian cultures.
- Learn some fundamental Creole or Patois phrases to interact with the community and demonstrate your respect for their culture. The words "good morning" (bonjour), "thank you" (merci), and "how are you?" (kijan ou ye?) are some of the more typical expressions.

- Take part in regional festivals and cultural events, including Carnival, to learn more about the culture and history of the island.
- Spend some time learning about the history of the island, especially its role as a colonial outpost and the lingering effects of slavery, and be sensitive to its ongoing social and economic difficulties.

Keep recycling and waste in mind:

St. John is a tiny island with few options for recycling and waste disposal. Here are some suggestions to lessen your effect and keep the island tidy:

- Steer clear of single-use plastic items including cutlery, straws, and cups. Bring your own bags, utensils, and reusable water bottles instead.
- Put recycling and trash in the appropriate bins, and refrain from leaving any litter.
- While you're there, think about helping out with beach clean-ups or other environmental conservation initiatives.

Keep up with news, safety, and security:

As with any trip, it's necessary to be aware of current affairs and security threats. The following resources can assist you in staying current:

- For the most recent travel warnings and updates, visit the USVI Department of Tourism website.
- Keep up with neighborhood news sources and social media profiles to learn about upcoming events and activities on the island.
- Be mindful of your surroundings and take the essential safety precautions, such as avoiding dark

locations at night and not leaving valuables unattended in public places, to keep yourself and others safe.

You may make your trip to St. John not only pleasurable but also responsible and considerate by remembering these extra suggestions. You may contribute to preserving the island's natural beauty for future generations to enjoy by patronizing local businesses and being aware of your impact on the environment and community.

Chapter 3: St. Thomas

Introduction to St. Thomas

The US Virgin Islands' second-largest island, St. Thomas, is situated in the eastern Caribbean Sea. It has a population of about 52,000 people and a land area of 31 square miles (80 square kilometers). Tourists from all over the world frequent St. Thomas because of its stunning beaches, warm tropical atmosphere, and historical sites.

There are numerous direct flights from significant cities in the United States, Canada, and Europe to St. Thomas, making travel there rather simple. Several sizable airlines fly into the Cyril E. King International Airport, which is situated on the island's southwest coast. Additionally, travelers can go to St. Thomas by cruise ship from busy ports like Miami and San Juan or by ferry from nearby islands like St. John, St. Croix, and the British Virgin Islands.

St. Thomas is best visited between December and April, when the weather is bright and dry and the average high is 80°F (27°C). However, this is also peak season, which means more people and more expensive costs. Although the temperature could be a little bit warmer and more humid, the shoulder season, which runs from May to August, can be a fantastic time to visit for cheaper rates and less tourists. Visitors should be aware of the possibility of tropical storms and make preparations accordingly between June and November, which is hurricane season in the Caribbean.

Renting a car makes getting around St. Thomas easier because there are few public transportation options and taxi fares can be high. In the capital city of the US Virgin Islands, Charlotte Amalie, visitors can rent a car either at the airport or downtown. However, St. Thomas's winding, winding roads and steep hills can make driving difficult. Another way to get around is by taxi, although the cost can mount up quickly, especially if you're traveling in a group.

Each and every kind of traveler will find something appealing on the lovely and diversified island of St. Thomas. St. Thomas is certain to make an impression, whether you're looking for adventure, relaxation, or cultural immersion.

Overview of the island's geography, history, and culture

Geography:

Along with St. Croix and St. John, St. Thomas is one of the three main islands that make up the US Virgin Islands. It is situated in the Caribbean Sea, south of the British Virgin Islands and east of Puerto Rico. The overall land area of St. Thomas is only 31 square miles (80 square kilometers), making it a comparatively small island. It has a rough, rocky environment, with Crown Mountain, at 1,556 feet (474 meters above sea level), being the highest point. Beautiful beaches, crystal-clear sea, and luxuriant tropical foliage are all hallmarks of St. Thomas.

History:

St. Thomas has a lengthy and interesting past. The Ciboney people were the first to live on the island, followed by the Arawaks and finally the Caribs. On his second trip to the

Americas, Christopher Columbus visited the island in 1493 and gave it the name St. Thomas. As numerous European nations fought for possession of the island, St. Thomas served as a trade post for items including sugar, rum, and other commodities in the next decades. St. Thomas and the other US Virgin Islands were acquired from Denmark in 1917, and both became a part of the US.

Culture:

The history and topography of St. Thomas have influenced the city's dynamic and diversified culture. There are about 50,000 people living on the island, with a mixture of African, European, and Caribbean influences. Spanish and Creole are also spoken in addition to English, which is the official language. Calypso, reggae, and steel drum music are popular genres in St. Thomas' vibrant music scene. The island also has a vibrant culinary tradition that frequently uses fish, Caribbean spices, and tropical fruits. On St. Thomas, Carnival is a significant celebration that includes vibrant parades, live music, and dance acts.

Travelers must be familiar with the island's geography, history, and culture in order to truly appreciate the island and its attractions. This summary can give tourists a better understanding of the character of the island and set the stage for the different experiences and activities they may have while touring St. Thomas.

Traveling to St. Thomas by cruise liner, ferry, or airplane

Plane:

The Cyril E. King International Airport (STT), which is located in St. Thomas, is serviced by direct flights from a number of US destinations, including Atlanta, Charlotte, Miami, and New York. There is a chance that international flights from Canada and Europe will stopover in other US locations. Approximately 4 miles from Charlotte Amalie, the airport is situated on the western side of the island.

Pros:

- The quickest method of transportation, with aircraft available from numerous major US cities
- An accommodating and practical choice, especially for time-pressed travelers
- To accommodate various travel budgets, airline carriers provide a variety of fare classes.

Cons:

- Could cost more than using a boat or cruise ship
- There are baggage limits.
- Travel time may increase due to security procedures and boarding times.

Ferry:

By ferry, the US Virgin Islands and British Virgin Islands are easily accessible from St. Thomas. Between St. Thomas and St. John, St. Croix, Water Island, and Tortola, ferries are run by a number of businesses, including Native Son, Inter-Island, and Varlack Ventures.

Pros:

- An alternate that is less expensive than flying
- A scenic and fun mode of transportation that offers breathtaking views of the Caribbean Sea and the nearby islands
- Generally trustworthy and prompt service

Cons:

- Is more time-consuming than flying, and ferry schedules might not be as frequent as plane schedules
- The weather can affect ferry service
- May be crowded, especially during periods of heavy travel

Cruise Ship:

Carnival, Royal Caribbean, Norwegian, and Disney are just a few of the Caribbean-based cruise lines that frequently call at St. Thomas. At the West Indian Company Dock in Charlotte Amalie, cruise ships can dock.

Pros:

- A budget-friendly choice, especially for tourists who want to visit several Caribbean locations
- All-inclusive experience including meals, entertainment, and activities while traveling
- Excellent for parties, families, and couples traveling together.

Cons:

- Short stay on the island because most cruise ships only dock there for one or two days
- During the busiest cruise season, crowded tourist destinations
- It might not be as immersive an experience as spending a lot of time on the island.

Whether you decide to use a flight, a ferry, or a cruise ship to get to St. Thomas, each means of transportation has pros and cons. When determining which choice is best for you, take into account your preferences for travel, time, and budget.

Best time to visit St. Thomas for optimal weather and events

Due to its warm tropical environment and picturesque surroundings, St. Thomas is a well-liked vacation spot all year round. Nevertheless, depending on what you want out of your vacation experience, some seasons of the year could be better than others.

The winter months of December through March are the greatest times to visit St. Thomas for the best weather. The humidity is generally low and temperatures during this period range from the mid-70s to the mid-80s Fahrenheit. In the Virgin Islands, this is also the driest and least likely time of year for rain. With such excellent weather, now is the ideal time to take advantage of St. Thomas's stunning beaches and outdoor pursuits like hiking, scuba diving, and snorkeling.

In addition to having pleasant weather during the winter, St. Thomas also offers a number of well-attended events. The St. Thomas Carnival, which takes place in late April or early May, is the most well-known of these occasions. This carnival, which involves parades, music, dancing, and food, is a vibrant celebration of the island's culture.

The best time to visit St. Thomas, however, is from May through September if you want to save money and stay away from the crowds. Since this is regarded as the off-season, hotel and flight costs are typically lower than they are during the busy season. Travelers should be aware that this is hurricane season in the Caribbean, so they should monitor weather reports and think about getting travel insurance.

The number of visitors should also be taken into account while choosing the optimum time to visit St. Thomas. During the summer and around vacations and school breaks, St. Thomas, a well-liked cruise port, may become fairly congested. Consider traveling in April/May or October/November, which are the shoulder seasons, if you wish to avoid crowded areas. The weather is still beautiful during these months, and there are less visitors.

It's also important to keep in mind that while St. Thomas is always warm, the summer months of June through August may be particularly hot and humid. This can be a terrific season to go if you don't mind the heat and humidity, especially if you want to enjoy water activities like swimming, snorkeling, and boating.

The high travel season on the island should also be taken into account when choosing the optimum time to visit St. Thomas. This typically lasts from mid-December to mid-April, when a large number of visitors arrive on the island to escape the chilly winters on the American mainland. Hotel and rental prices are at their greatest during this period, and popular sites and beaches may be very crowded. To get the greatest deals and prevent disappointment, plan your trip during high season and reserve your lodging and activities well in advance.

The winter months of December through March are the finest for weather and events in St. Thomas, while May through September is the off-season with cheaper pricing and less crowding. When making travel plans to St. Thomas, visitors should also take into account variables like weather, humidity, crowds, and peak season. The ideal time to visit ultimately depends on your individual preferences and travel priorities.

Tips for getting around the island, including rental cars and taxis

Getting around St. Thomas is necessary to fully explore and take advantage of everything it has to offer. The following advice will help you navigate St. Thomas:

Renting a car:

The most popular method of transportation in St. Thomas is automobile rental. On the island, there are a number of automobile rental agencies; the majority are either at the Cyril E. King Airport or in the neighboring city of Charlotte Amalie. Although the island has a solid network of roads and highways, some of them can be winding and small, so it's vital to drive carefully. It's also important to remember that in St. Thomas, the left side of the road is used for driving.

Taxis:

On St. Thomas, taxis are easily accessible, especially in well-known tourist locales like Charlotte Amalie and close to the cruise ship port. Make cautious to clarify the pricing before boarding a taxi because they operate on a fixed fare basis. If you're traveling in a group, sharing a taxi with another passenger can be a cost-effective solution.

Using Public transportation:

"Safaris," open-air buses that run on set routes, are the only mode of public transit in St. Thomas. Although cheap, safaris might be crowded and lack air conditioning and much solitude. Safaris can be a fun and exciting way to travel around if you're familiar with the local transit and want to experience the island like a local.

Cycling and walking:

Certain parts of St. Thomas, like the center of Charlotte Amalie, are conveniently walkable. Another option is biking, especially in the districts close to the beaches. However, keep in mind that St. Thomas has a mountainous topography and that it may become rather hot there, so remember to drink enough of water and wear sunscreen.

Your tastes, financial situation, and travel plans will determine the appropriate means of transportation. Compared to taxis and public transportation, renting a car offers the most flexibility and independence and is recommended for one-time or short-distance journeys. Planning ahead is advised if you intend to hire a car in St. Thomas because parking can be difficult in some areas, especially in the downtown regions.

Top Attractions and Activities

The US Virgin Islands' St. Thomas is a stunning and lively island with a variety of intriguing sights and things to do. The following are some of the main sights and activities on St. Thomas:

Skyride to Paradise Point:

Popular in St. Thomas, the Skyride to Paradise Point provides breathtaking views of the island and the surrounding Caribbean Sea. Visitors can take a cable car to the summit of the mountain, where they can dine in the restaurant or peruse the gift shop while taking in the panoramic views of the island. The Skyride is a fantastic opportunity to see St. Thomas' natural beauty from a different angle.

Frenchtown:

On the western side of Charlotte Amalie, Frenchtown is a historic district. The region was colonized by French and Danish inhabitants at the beginning of the 18th century, and it still has a lot of its original charm. Visitors can stroll through the winding streets and colorful homes, indulge in regional cuisine at one of the numerous cafes and restaurants, or discover more about the region's history at the French Heritage Museum.

Water Island:

A little island called Water Island is situated not far from St. Thomas' coast. The island is renowned for its immaculate beaches, glistening waters, and laid-back vibe. From St. Thomas, visitors can take a ferry to Water Island, where they can spend the day kayaking, swimming, or snorkeling. On the island, there are a few eateries and bars where guests may grab a bite to eat or unwind with a tropical beverage.

Magen's Bay Arboretum and Botanical Garden:

The Magen's Bay Arboretum and Botanical Garden is a stunning paradise of tropical plants and flowers that is close to Magen's Bay. The gardens are open for visitors to stroll through and discover the numerous plant types that flourish on the island. Additionally, there are hiking routes that meander through the gardens and provide breathtaking views of the harbor and the nearby hills.

Coral Reef National Monument:

Off the coast of St. Thomas is the Coral Reef National Monument, a marine protected area. Coral, fish, and sea turtles are among the many different types of aquatic life that call the monument home. On a boat tour of the monument, visitors can snorkel or scuba dive among the colorful coral reefs. Anyone interested in maritime conservation and the preservation of natural environments must visit the monument.

Honeymoon Beach:

A quick ferry ride from St. Thomas will take you to Water Island's quiet Honeymoon Beach. The sand is soft and white, and the water is tranquil and clear at the beach. Visitors can rent beach umbrellas and chairs, go snorkeling, or just unwind and enjoy the sunshine. Additionally, there is a beach bar and restaurant where guests can get something to eat and sip on a tropical drink.

Drake's Seat:

The picturesque vantage point known as Drake's Seat is situated on St. Thomas' western side. The neighboring hillsides and Magen's Bay are beautifully visible from the viewpoint. Visitors can ascend the hill to the top to admire the expansive vistas or to take pictures of the stunning scenery. There are also many hiking paths in the area, which run through the slopes and provide even more breathtaking views of the island.

St. Thomas Synagogue:

Anyone interested in Jewish history and culture must visit the St. Thomas Synagogue, one of the oldest synagogues in the Western Hemisphere. The 1830s saw the construction of the synagogue, which has lovely architectural characteristics and a lengthy past. The history of the Jewish community on

St. Thomas can be learned by taking a guided tour of the synagogue.

Bluebeard's Castle:

In Charlotte Amalie, there is a historical site called Bluebeard's Castle. In order to guard the town against pirates and other intruders, the castle was constructed in the 17th century as a watchtower. The castle is now a well-liked tourist destination with lovely grounds, a dining area, and a museum dedicated to pirates. The castle can be explored by guests, who can also discover its intriguing past.

Parasailing:

Parasailing is a well-liked pastime on St. Thomas for those seeking an exhilarating adventure. A guided parasailing excursion allows visitors to soar above the island and take in breath-taking vistas of the Caribbean Sea and the nearby islands. It will undoubtedly be a memorable experience and a wonderful chance to view the island from a different angle.

St. Thomas is a lively, interesting city with something to offer everyone. St. Thomas is the ideal location for exploration and discovery, regardless of your interests in history, culture, environment, or adventure.

Top Beaches

Some of the Caribbean's most stunning beaches may be found on St. Thomas. There is a beach on the island that will meet your needs, whether you're seeking for a busy environment with lots of services or a remote location for calm enjoyment. Here is a basic rundown of St. Thomas' top beaches:

Magens Bay:

The most well-known beach on St. Thomas is Magens Bay, and with good reason. It is one of the most stunning beaches in the world with a mile-long expanse of white sand and turquoise water. The beach sits on the island's north side and is reachable by automobile or taxi. The minimal entrance fee to the beach is justified given the amenities offered. On-site amenities include beach chairs, umbrellas, a snack bar, and kayaks and paddleboards for hire.

The tranquil waters of Magens Bay are one of the factors contributing to its popularity. Because of the coral reef that guards the bay, the waves are usually minimal and the water is tranquil. It is a fantastic swimming location as a result, especially for families with young children.

Lindquist Beach:

On St. Thomas' eastern coast, Lindquist Beach is a well-kept secret. It's a little more difficult to reach than some of the other beaches on the island, but the tranquil setting and breathtaking natural beauty make the journey worthwhile. There are no facilities on site, so bring your own beach supplies and food. The beach is reachable by walk or automobile (parking is a little fee).

The water at Lindquist Beach is incredibly clean, which is one of its unique features. It's an excellent place for swimming and snorkeling because the water is calm and shallow. It's a perfect place for a picnic or a quiet day of leisure because there is ample of white sand to sprawl out on.

Sapphire Beach:

On the east side of St. Thomas, Sapphire Beach is reachable by automobile or taxi. It's a busy beach with lots of facilities and things to do. Along with renting water sports equipment like jet skis and paddleboards, you may also hire beach chairs and umbrellas. Additionally, there are pubs and eateries close by where you can have a bite to eat or a refreshing beverage while basking in the sun.

Coral formations are one of Sapphire Beach's distinctive qualities. Due to the coral reef's proximity to the shore, snorkelers can witness a variety of fish and other marine life there. You can also take a glass-bottom boat excursion to see the underwater environment if you don't like snorkeling.

Secret Harbor Beach:

On the eastern part of St. Thomas, close to Red Hook, is Secret Harbor Beach. Despite being a little bit smaller than some of the island's other beaches, this one is nevertheless a fantastic place for swimming, snorkeling, and relaxation. The beach is next to a small resort and is reachable by automobile. On-site amenities include a restaurant, a bar, beach chairs, umbrellas, and water sport rentals.

The coral reef at Secret Harbor Beach is one of its unique features. Just offshore is the reef, which is a fantastic place for snorkeling and scuba diving. To independently explore the bay, you can also rent a paddleboard or a kayak.

The best beaches in St. Thomas have amenities for everyone, including white sand, coral reefs, and water sports in addition to calm waters. There is a beach on St. Thomas that will suit your needs, whether you're looking for a busy scene or a peaceful place to unwind.

Dining and Nightlife

St. Thomas has a wide variety of restaurants, serving anything from world cuisine to regional Caribbean food. Fresh seafood, tropical fruits, and spicy spices are common ingredients in many cuisines. Rum, the Caribbean's national spirit, is also used in a variety of cocktails.

.

Overview of St. Thomas's dining scene

The cuisine of St. Thomas reflects the island's multiculturalism. The island's rich culinary history reflects the influences of indigenous, European, and African cultures. The end result is a wide variety of tastes and cuisines that will appeal to all palates.

Trying the native cuisine is one of the best parts about dining in St. Thomas. Among the most well-liked regional dishes are:

In several eateries and pubs all across St. Thomas, conch fritters are a traditional Caribbean starter. The Caribbean is home to many conches, a kind of marine snail whose meat is frequently used in regional cooking. The meat is minced finely and combined with flour, egg, and seasonings to form conch fritters. After that, spoonfuls of the mixture are dropped into the hot oil and deep-fried till golden brown. Conch fritters are a tasty and well-liked snack in St. Thomas and are often served with a dipping sauce, such as tartar sauce or spicy sauce.

A mainstay of Caribbean cooking, johnnycakes are frequently served for breakfast or as a side dish with other meals. They are little, round, deep-fried cakes made of cornmeal, flour, and various other things like sugar and baking powder. The cakes are frequently served with butter and syrup and are typically crispy on the outside and soft on the inside. They can also be consumed without any toppings or with salty ones like cheese or bacon.

A typical Caribbean meal called saltfish is created from salted and dried cod. Before the fish is boiled and sautéed with onions, peppers, and tomatoes, it is given a quick rehydration by soaking it in water. The dish is a well-liked breakfast or brunch option in St. Thomas and is frequently served with johnnycakes or fried plantains. Other foods like fish cakes and stews frequently contain saltfish as an ingredient.

Visitors to St. Thomas may also want to taste the following other well-known dishes:

- Callaloo: A typical Caribbean stew made with leafy greens, coconut milk, and occasionally meat or shellfish. It frequently comes with beans and rice.
- Jerk chicken: A tasty and hot dish of marinated chicken that is grilled or smoked over wood.
- Roti is a flatbread that can be stuffed with curried meat, chicken, or vegetables. It is a well-liked street snack in St. Thomas and is available in markets and food trucks.
- Mango chutney: A sauce made from mangoes, vinegar, sugar, and spices. It is sweet and sour. It frequently goes with dishes of meat or shellfish as a condiment.

Visitors to St. Thomas can find a wide variety of international cuisines in addition to local fare. There are many American-style eateries and fast-food businesses on the island, along with popular cuisines including Italian, Asian, and Mexican.

St. Thomas features a number of food trucks and outdoor markets providing regional snacks and street food for people looking for a more casual eating experience. These are a fantastic choice for people on a tight budget or seeking a fast snack. Cuzzin's Caribbean Restaurant, which offers a variety of regional dishes, and Lattes in Paradise, which focuses on coffee and pastries, are two of the most well-known food trucks on St. Thomas.

In conclusion, there are many dining options in St. Thomas, ranging from international cuisine to local fare, from fine dining to fast food joints and street food. The dining scene in St. Thomas has something for everyone, whether you want to go out or remain with the tried-and-true.

Recommendations for seafood restaurants, casual eateries, and fine dining establishments

Seafood restaurants:

There are numerous top-notch seafood restaurants on the island of St. Thomas, which is renowned for its superb fresh seafood. These eateries serve a broad variety of seafood meals, frequently in classic Caribbean ways, including fish, lobster, and conch. Popular seafood restaurant Hook Line & Sinker serves a range of seafood delicacies, such as grilled fish, conch chowder, and lobster tail. Another excellent choice is the Twisted Cork Cafe, which offers fresh fish and foods from the neighborhood. A popular seafood restaurant in St. Thomas, Oceana offers mouthwatering ocean views and a menu full of seafood and steak delicacies.

Casual restaurants:

There are several informal restaurants in St. Thomas that provide great culinary choices and a laid-back atmosphere. These restaurants are ideal for a fast snack or a casual dinner, and they frequently serve regional delicacies such as rotis, patties, and johnnycakes. Locals and visitors alike enjoy Gladys' Cafe, which serves breakfast and lunch in the Caribbean style. Senor Pizza gives patrons scrumptious pizza and other Italian classics, and The Smoking Rooster delivers savory barbecue and pub fare.

Fine dining establishments:

St. Thomas features a number of fine dining venues that provide superb cuisine, first-rate service, and breathtaking vistas for those seeking a more affluent dining experience. These eateries are ideal for celebrations, date nights, or just treating yourself to a memorable meal. One of St. Thomas's most well-liked fine dining establishments, Old Stone Farmhouse offers a seasonal cuisine that emphasizes regional flavors and ingredients. Another excellent choice for great dining is Room with a View, which is perched on a hilltop and offers stunning views of Charlotte Amalie port. Also highly recommended is Mafolie Restaurant, which serves fusion Caribbean and international food and has a gorgeous view of the island.

From simple cafes to premium fine dining venues, St. Thomas visitors can choose from a variety of dining options. Fresh seafood is a particular highlight of the island, and there are a number of well respected seafood restaurants that serve up delectable delicacies. Visitors can enjoy the island's casual cafes for a more laid-back eating experience, while those looking for a special dinner can select from one of St. Thomas's well regarded fine dining venues.

Tips for nightlife on St. Thomas

Whether you're searching for a simple drink or a night of dancing, St. Thomas has a thriving nightlife scene with something for everyone. Here are some pointers on where to go out on the island at night:

Lounges and bars:

There are several bars and lounges in St. Thomas where you can unwind and have a drink, frequently with live music playing in the background. Popular restaurant Duffy's Love Shack is well-known for its vibrant interior design and inventive drinks. Another favorite is The Fat Turtle, which has a lively environment and a variety of drink specials. On the island there is also a Hooters for those seeking a more familiar experience.

Clubs and Dance Venues:

There are many clubs and dance venues in St. Thomas to pick from if you're in the mood to dance. A DJ spins tunes at the Red Hook Dive Center all night long, making it a popular place for dancing. Another choice is The Shipwreck Tavern, which features a dance floor and a combination of live music and DJ sessions.

Live Music Venues:

On St. Thomas, there are numerous venues where visitors can listen to live music performed by regional musicians and bands. Favorite places to hear a fusion of country, rock, and reggae music include The Caribbean Saloon. Another well-liked location is Tickles Dockside Pub, which is renowned for its waterfront setting and live music. Island Time Pub is a more recent addition to the island's entertainment scene. It has an outdoor stage where local musicians frequently perform.

Happy Hour Specials:

On St. Thomas, a lot of bars and eateries offer happy hour promotions, making it a fantastic time to check out new locations while saving money. These promotions, which feature reduced prices on drinks and snacks, usually run in the late afternoon or early evening.

Beach Bars:

Visit one of St. Thomas' many beach bars for a more laid-back setting. These bars provide a relaxed atmosphere with fantastic views and are frequently found directly on the beach. On the east end of the island are two well-liked beach bars: Dinghy's Beach Bar & Grill and Magen's Bay Beach Bar, which provides breathtaking views of one of the island's most well-liked beaches.

Special Events:

St. Thomas has a number of special events all year long that provide a distinctive evening experience. The Carnival event, which takes place in April or May and includes parades, music, and a lot of dancing, is one of the most well-liked. Themed parties in neighborhood bars and clubs are another event to keep an eye out for.

The nightlife in St. Thomas is vibrant and diversified, with something for everyone. On this lovely Caribbean island, you're likely to find what you're looking for, whether you're looking for a leisurely drink, a fun night out dancing, or some live music.

In conclusion, St. Thomas has a vibrant nightlife and a variety of dining alternatives, including both casual and fine dining restaurants, as well as local and international cuisine. St. Thomas is a terrific destination for individuals wishing to unwind and have fun because visitors can take advantage of a selection of bars, clubs, and live music venues.

Where to Stay

There are many options available to you when it comes to selecting the ideal lodging for your stay on St. Thomas, ranging from opulent villas to cost-effective alternatives. What to anticipate in each category is more fully explained below:

Overview of the Accommodations in St. Thomas

St. Thomas provides a wide variety of lodging options to accommodate all tastes and price ranges. The three major forms of lodging on the island are further described as follows:

Hotels:

There are several hotels in St. Thomas, from big chain hotels to more modest boutique lodgings. The majority of the island's hotels have amenities like restaurants, swimming pools, and concierge services. Some of the more opulent hotels feature spa services and private beaches. There are also smaller hotels that offer a more intimate and personal setting for individuals who prefer a more low-key experience.

Resorts:

There are a number of resorts in St. Thomas that include all-inclusive packages, exclusive beaches, and a variety of eating options. Additionally, some resorts provide spa facilities, golf courses, and other leisure pursuits. Many of the island's major resorts are situated right on the beach and provide a variety of water sports and other outdoor activities. There are private pools and lounges at several resorts for those seeking a more tranquil experience.

Vacation Rentals:

Vacation rentals are a terrific alternative if you're searching for something more exclusive and autonomous. There are many different types of vacation rentals available in St. Thomas, including condos, private homes, and apartments. As they frequently provide greater room and facilities than hotels or resorts, vacation rentals might be a more cost-effective choice for families or groups of friends. For individuals who like to prepare their own meals while on vacation and have more control over their itinerary, vacation rentals can be a fantastic option.

Recommendations for Accommodations

Depending on your travel tastes and budget, there are different lodging alternatives available for your vacation to St. Thomas. The different suggestions for accommodations listed in the guide are broken down as follows:

Luxury Properties:

There are some of the most opulent properties in the Caribbean on St. Thomas if you want to splash out and have an opulent experience. These facilities frequently provide first-rate amenities including private beaches, fine dining, spa services, and breathtaking vistas. Here are a few of the island's finest luxurious homes:

- The Ritz Carlton: Located on Great Bay, this opulent hotel provides breath-taking views of the Caribbean Sea. There are 180 guest rooms, a spa, a fitness center, many dining options, and a private beach at the hotel.
- The St. Regis: This five-star resort is situated on St. John's Bay's immaculate beach and offers visitors opulent lodgings, individualized butler service, and top-notch amenities, such as an infinity pool, spa services, and an on-site restaurant.
- The Frenchman's Reef Marriott: This opulent hotel offers breath-taking views of the ocean and opulent extras like an infinity pool, spa services, a private beach, and a variety of dining options.

Family-Friendly Resorts:

Families should visit St. Thomas since there are several resorts that cater to families and have amenities and activities for children of all ages. These resorts frequently offer family-friendly amenities including water parks and kids' clubs. Top family-friendly resorts to take into account are listed below:

- Sugar Bay Resort and Spa: Located on St. Thomas' eastern coast, this all-inclusive resort has a range of family-friendly activities like kayaking, paddleboarding, snorkeling, and more. A kids' club, teen lounge, and a water park with a slide are all available at the resort.
- Bolongo Bay Beach Resort: This resort is noted for its amiable staff and family-friendly activities, including water sports, volleyball, and live entertainment. It is situated on a lovely beach on St. Thomas' southern coast. A family-friendly restaurant, game room, and kids' club are also available at the resort.
- Marriott's Frenchman's Cove: Perfect for families, this resort offers roomy villas with full kitchens and separate living spaces. Along with a kids club, a family-friendly pool with a waterslide, and a variety of sports including kayaking and snorkeling, the resort also offers.

Budget-Friendly Options:

St. Thomas offers a variety of inexpensive lodging options if you're on a tight budget. Smaller hotels, guesthouses, and hostels are some of these choices. Here are some well-liked inexpensive choices on the island:

- The Windward Passage Hotel is a budget-friendly hotel with comfortable amenities that is centrally located in Charlotte Amalie. A restaurant and a fitness facility are also features of the hotel.

- Galleon House: This lovely inn on Government Hill in Charlotte Amalie provides reasonably priced lodging with a vintage vibe. Additionally, the guesthouse features a rooftop terrace with breathtaking views.
- Emerald Beach Resort: This beachfront resort is close to the airport and offers reasonably priced lodging. In addition to a restaurant and bar, the resort features a pool and access to the beach.

St. Thomas boasts a wide range of lodging alternatives, whether you're seeking for opulent, family-friendly, or affordable options. Choosing your lodging should take into account your travel interests and budget, and the suggestions above can assist you in locating the ideal lodging for your visit to St. Thomas.

Tips for Choosing the Best Location

It's crucial to consider the activities and sites you wish to experience during your trip when deciding where to stay on St. Thomas. Following are some pointers for picking the ideal place in light of your interests:

Proximity to the Beach:

If you adore the beach, you should pick lodgings that are close to the water in St. Thomas, which has some of the most gorgeous beaches in the Caribbean. Magens Bay, Lindquist Beach, and Sapphire Beach are a few of the best beaches on the island. If you stay close to the beach, you may spend your days swimming in the clear waters, sunbathing on the sand, and participating in water sports like snorkeling or paddleboarding. It's simple to discover a place that meets your needs on St. Thomas because so many lodging options offer beachfront access or are close to the beach.

Proximity to Shopping:

Additionally, St. Thomas is well-known for its shopping, especially in Charlotte Amalie, the island's capital. If you want to indulge in some retail therapy while on vacation, pick lodgings that are situated in or close to Charlotte Amalie. There are many stores, marketplaces, and boutiques in the region that provide anything from high-end jewelry and fashionable clothes to regional crafts and mementos. If you stay in Charlotte Amalie, you can travel to other shopping districts on the island by short taxi ride or by walking to the shops.

Proximity to Nightlife:

You should pick lodging close to the pubs and clubs if you want to experience St. Thomas's vibrant nightlife. On the island, Hooters, The Beach Bar, and Duffy's Love Shack are a few of the best places to go out at night. You may easily walk or take a short taxi journey to enjoy a night out on the town if you stay anywhere close to these locations. However, it's recommended to select hotels that are far from the districts with a lot of nightlife if you like a more tranquil and serene atmosphere.

There are a few other things to take into account while deciding where to stay on St. Thomas. Here are some extra pointers:

Budget:

St. Thomas provides a variety of lodging options, from high-end resorts to inexpensive motels and rental homes, to meet different spending ranges. A vacation rental or hostel can be a better alternative for you to stay in if you're traveling on a tight budget than a typical hotel. On the other hand, if you're searching for an opulent experience, you may pick from some of the island's best hotels and resorts.

Transportation:

When deciding where to stay, it's crucial to think about how you'll navigate the island. If you intend to rent a car, you might want to select lodgings with free or inexpensive parking. As an alternative, you could choose to pick accommodations that are close to bus stops or taxi stands if you prefer to rely on public transportation or taxis.

Amenities:

Finally, think about the amenities that are important to you while selecting a place to stay. While some lodgings provide more basic amenities, others may have on-site dining options, swimming pools, exercise centers, and spas. Consider what's most essential to you and pick accommodations with the features you want.

Your trip's outcome may be greatly influenced by the lodging you select on St. Thomas. You can select the ideal lodging for your stay on the island by taking your travel choices, spending capacity, transit requirements, and desired facilities into account.

Overall, St. Thomas offers a wide range of lodging choices; the one you pick will depend on your preferences and financial situation.

In conclusion, St. Thomas is a must-visit destination for visitors to the US Virgin Islands, with plenty of attractions, beaches, dining options, and lodging to suit all tastes and budgets. Consider your priorities, whether it's luxury, family-friendly amenities, proximity to the beach, or nightlife, and then choose the accommodation that best fits your needs. St.

Thomas offers something to offer every traveler, whether they are looking for excitement, relaxation, or a little bit of both.

Chapter 4: Exploring the USVI

The US Virgin Islands are a popular place to travel because of their breathtaking natural beauty and fascinating history. This chapter will walk you through some of the top sights to see and things to do in the US Virgin Islands, such as national parks, historic sites, outdoor activities, and island hopping.

National Parks and Historic Sites

The three national parks in the territory are outstanding examples of how the US Virgin Islands are renowned for their breathtaking natural beauty and rich cultural history.

St. John's Virgin Islands National Park is one of the USVI's crown jewels. The park, which occupies two-thirds of the island, has more than 20 hiking paths, each of which offers a different perspective of the island's verdant landscape, gushing waterfalls, and picture-perfect beaches. The Reef Bay Trail, which meanders through the forest and passes historic ruin sites including sugar mills and plantation homes, is one of the most well-liked routes. In addition, the park is home to Trunk Bay and Cinnamon Bay, two of the top snorkeling and scuba diving locations in the USVI. Visitors can swim with stingrays and sea turtles while exploring vibrant coral reefs and other marine life.

A unique look into the USVI's colonial past may be found at Christiansted National Historic Site on St. Croix. The area is home to a number of ancient structures, notably Fort Christiansvaern, which the Danes constructed in the 1700s to defend the island against pirates and invaders. Visitors can take guided tours of the structures and discover more about the island's history, from the first European settlers' arrival to the difficulties of the slaves who labored on the island's sugar fields. Traditional dance and music performances are among the cultural demonstrations and events held at the location.

A special location that blends natural and cultural history is Salt River Bay National Historical Park and Ecological Preserve on St. Croix. A stunning mangrove ecology, which supports a variety of avian and marine species, including the critically endangered brown pelican, may be found in the park. Visitors can learn about the significance of these ecosystems to the health of the ocean by paddling a kayak or a stand-up paddleboard through the mangroves. A significant cultural landmark in the park is the spot where Christopher Columbus set foot during his second trip to the New World. In addition to learning about the difficulties of the native peoples and enslaved Africans who helped create the history of the USVI, visitors can explore the ruins of the Taino people who lived on the island before European settlers arrived.

The US Virgin Islands' national parks and historical sites also present a chance to engage with the local population and promote sustainable tourism. Many of the parks and sites collaborate closely with neighborhood businesses and groups to advance conservation initiatives and safeguard the region's distinctive cultural history. To learn more about the colorful culture of the USVI and to support the local economy, tourists can also explore the adjacent towns and neighborhoods, sample the cuisine, and shop for handcrafted goods and souvenirs.

The US Virgin Islands' national parks and historical monuments are also fantastic places to spread the word about responsible tourism and eco-friendly travel. The parks and sites have put in place a variety of sustainability measures, from trash reduction and energy conservation to the preservation of endangered species and ecosystems. By abiding by the park's rules and regulations, reducing their environmental impact, and leaving the region in better condition than they found it, visitors can contribute.

Anyone interested in environment, history, or culture should visit the national parks and historical sites of the US Virgin Islands. There is fun for everyone, from guided tours and cultural events to hiking and water sports. Visitors may engage with the local culture, promote sustainable travel, and discover the rich history of the USVI, all of which contribute to an amazing experience.

Watersports and Outdoor Activities

The US Virgin Islands are a favourite vacation spot for lovers of watersports thanks to their well-known for having pristine seas and a plethora of marine life. There are several possibilities to enjoy kayaking, paddleboarding, scuba diving, and snorkeling, and each island has a choice of outfitters and tour providers.

Snorkeling and Scuba Diving
Due to its beautiful, warm waters and tremendous diversity of marine life, the US Virgin Islands are recognized as one of the best places in the Caribbean for snorkeling and scuba diving. Divers and snorkelers of all skill levels will find

something to enjoy in the USVI, from coral gardens to underwater caves and shipwrecks.

Snorkeling:

In the USVI, snorkeling is a well-liked activity because several reefs are reachable right from the shore. Trunk Bay on St. John is one of the most well-known snorkeling locations in the USVI. It has a 225-yard underwater trail that offers a self-guided tour of the reef and includes underwater signage that describe the various fish and coral species. Another well-liked location for snorkeling on St. John is Cinnamon Bay, which has a long, broad reef that is simple to reach from the shore.

Buck Island on St. Croix, which the US government has designated a National Monument for because of its magnificent coral reef system, is yet another fantastic snorkeling location. Snorkelers can go through a series of coral formations on the underwater route at Buck Island, which is home to a broad range of marine life, including sea turtles, rays, and schools of vibrant tropical fish.

Coral World Ocean Park on St. Thomas provides a special opportunity to get up close with marine life, including sea turtles, sharks, and rays, for those who want a more structured experience. In a sizable, enclosed area with reproductions of several Caribbean environments, such as a coral reef and a mangrove lagoon, visitors can enjoy snorkeling.

Scuba diving

In the USVI, scuba diving is also very well-liked, and there are lots of licensed dive companies who provide a variety of experiences for divers of all skill levels. The Wreck of the Rhone on Salt Island, which gained notoriety thanks to the film "The Deep," is one of the most well-known diving sites in the USVI. The Rhone was a British mail steamer that sank in 1867 during a cyclone; today, a variety of marine species, including barracudas, jacks, and angelfish, call the ruin home.

Carvel Rock on St. John, which is renowned for its stunning underwater topography and the sizable schools of pelagic fish that can be seen there, is another well-known dive location. For experienced divers, the dive site at Congo Cay on St. John is renowned for its steep walls that drop down to more than 90 feet, providing a singular and exhilarating experience.

Kayaking and Paddleboarding

In the US Virgin Islands, kayaking and paddleboarding are well-liked pastimes that provide tourists the chance to explore the magnificent shoreline and pristine waterways of the islands. Kayaking and stand-up paddleboarding offer a tranquil and pleasant way to take in the beauty of the USVI thanks to the quiet waters and stunning scenery.

Guided Kayak and Paddleboard Tours:

A lot of tour companies provide guided kayak and paddleboard tours, giving tourists a distinctive approach to explore the islands. The guides on these excursions frequently have knowledge of the local flora and wildlife as well as the history and culture of the islands.

Sunset Paddles:

The sunset paddle is one of the most well-liked kayak and paddleboard excursions. Visitors can watch the sun set over the horizon while paddling along the coastline on these cruises, which normally take place in the late afternoon or early evening. Paddles at sunset are a tranquil and romantic way to take in the beauty of the USVI.

Bioluminescent Bay Tours:

A bioluminescent bay trip offers another distinctive kayaking and paddleboarding experience in the US Virgin Islands. The bioluminescent plankton that resides in a number of USVI waters illuminates the water at night. These excursions, which usually begin after sunset, provide tourists a spectacular and unique experience.

Popular Kayaking and Paddleboarding Spots:

With tranquil seas and breathtaking views of the shoreline, Cane Bay on St. Croix is a well-liked location for kayaking and stand-up paddleboarding. Numerous marine species, such as sea turtles, rays, and vibrant fish, call the area home.

An additional popular location for kayaking and paddleboarding is Honeymoon Beach on St. John. The cove that protects the beach has calm waters perfect for paddling. Also accessible by kayak is the little island of Waterlemon Cay, which offers fantastic snorkeling.

In the US Virgin Islands, kayaking and paddleboarding are well-liked pastimes that give tourists a distinctive opportunity to explore the magnificent shoreline and pristine waterways of the islands. Every interest and skill level can be satisfied with a kayaking or paddleboarding experience thanks to guided tours, sunset paddles, and bioluminescent bay trips. A must-try activity in the USVI is kayaking or paddleboarding, regardless of your level of skill.

Sailing, Fishing, and Boating

Sailing, fishing, and boating enthusiasts will find a multitude of options in the US Virgin Islands. Many tour companies offer day outings and sunset cruises on sailboats and catamarans due to the perfect sailing conditions provided by the calm waters and consistent trade winds.

Sailing:

In the USVI, sailing is a well-liked hobby with lots of options for both novice and expert sailors. The protected bays and coves on the islands, along with the consistent trade winds, make for ideal sailing conditions. A lot of charter businesses provide half-day, full-day, and multi-day charters so that tourists can see the islands from various angles.

Just a short sail from St. Thomas, the British Virgin Islands are one of the most well-liked sailing locations in the USVI. The BVIs present a special chance to discover new islands and get a taste of other cultures.

Fishing:

The USVI offers year-round access to a variety of fish species, making fishing another well-liked pastime there. The islands provide a variety of fishing opportunities, including fly fishing on the flats and deep-sea fishing. For half-day or full-day fishing trips with the possibility of catching marlin, sailfish, tuna, and wahoo, there are numerous charter boats and guides available.

In the USVI, deep-sea fishing is particularly well-liked, with many charter boats leaving from the harbors and marinas of the islands. Some of the most sought-after game species in the area include the Wahoo, Blue Marlin, and Sailfish, and many anglers travel there from all over the world to try their luck.

Boating:

A lot of tourists choose to use boats to explore the bays, coves, and beaches of the US Virgin Islands. Renting a boat offers guests a variety of alternatives, including motorboats, sailboats, and catamarans, allowing them to tailor their boating experience to their own requirements.

There are additional possibilities for paddleboats and electric boats for those seeking a more distinctive boating experience. A lot of marinas and harbors provide boat tours that let guests explore the islands and the area around them with the aid of a knowledgeable guide.

The USVI provides a variety of possibilities for visitors to enjoy the sea, whether they are enthusiastic sailors, fisherman, or just want to cruise along the lovely coastline of the islands. The islands' calm waters and consistent trade winds allow for ideal sailing conditions, and the variety of fish species makes for thrilling fishing expeditions. Boat rentals and cruises provide a distinctive method to discover the natural beauty of the islands and give visitors a different viewpoint of the US Virgin Islands.

Adrenaline Activities

The USVI provides a variety of thrilling activities to get your heart racing if you're seeking for an adrenaline rush. Visitors can enjoy a variety of exhilarating activities in the islands, from zipping through the dense rainforest canopy to flying above the turquoise waters.

Zip-Lining:

Zip-lining through the canopy of the rainforest is one of the most thrilling ways to take in the splendor of the US Virgin Islands. Adventurers love to visit St. Thomas' Tree Limin'

Extreme zipline course because it provides sweeping aerial views of the island and the port. Six ziplines and two suspension bridges are part of the tour, which also offers expert commentary and safety instructions from qualified guides.

Parasailing:

Parasailing is a preferred activity in the US Virgin Islands for individuals who wish to soar above the water. While flying through the air, visitors may take in beautiful views of the coastline and the pristine oceans. On St. Croix, parasailing is an option with various operators providing tandem or solo rides. Both beginners and seasoned thrill-seekers can participate in the sport because safety gear and guidance are offered.

Other Adrenaline Activities:

There are a variety of additional heart-pounding activities to attempt in the US Virgin Islands in addition to zip-lining and parasailing. On the windy coasts of the island, visitors can try their hand at kiteboarding or windsurfing or go rock climbing on St. John's rugged cliffs. The islands provide a variety of tracks across the difficult terrain, with breathtaking views of the surroundings, for those who prefer mountain biking.

For tourists searching for an action-packed holiday, the USVI offers a variety of adrenaline-pumping activities. The islands offer a wide range of thrilling activities, such as zip-lining beneath the rainforest canopy and parasailing above the pristine waters. The USVI has activities for everyone, whether you're an experienced thrill-seeker or just looking to try something new.

The USVI offers a wide variety of outdoor experiences and activities for guests, regardless of whether they enjoy being on the water or want to stay on dry land. There is something for everyone to enjoy in the US Virgin Islands, from experiencing the breathtaking coral reefs while snorkeling or scuba diving to taking a tranquil kayak or paddleboard trip or even getting your heart racing with zip-lining or parasailing.

Island Hopping

In the US Virgin Islands, island hopping is a well-liked activity that lets tourists explore various islands and take in their individual charms and attractions. For further information on each of the three major islands, see:

St. Thomas:

The most developed and active of the three islands, St. Thomas has a buzzing environment and a ton of things to do to keep tourists occupied. The US Virgin Islands' capital, Charlotte Amalie, is situated on St. Thomas and has a wide range of dining, shopping, and nightlife opportunities. Visitors can meander through the vibrant streets of the Frenchtown area or visit historic places like the 17th-century Fort Christian. Visitors can ride the Skyride to Paradise Point for a bird's-eye view of the island and port. Magens Bay and Sapphire Beach are just two of St. Thomas' stunning beaches.

St. John:

St. John is renowned for its unhurried atmosphere and natural beauty. The Virgin Islands National Park, which has pristine beaches, hiking trails, and ancient ruins, protects two-thirds of the island. The park is open for self-guided exploration or for guided tours. Hawksnest Bay, Cinnamon

Bay, and Trunk Bay are a few of St. John's busiest beaches. The island also has a thriving artistic community, with studios and galleries showing the creations of regional artists.

St. Croix:

The largest of the three islands, St. Croix, is known for its extensive cultural heritage. On St. Croix, the ancient town of Christiansted is home to colonial-era buildings like the 18th-century Fort Christiansvaern. Visitors can explore the neighboring Buck Island Reef National Monument or take a walking tour of the town. Additionally well-known for its cuisine, St. Croix features a wide range of eateries that serve regional specialties including conch fritters and mango salsa. The Crucian Christmas Festival and the St. Croix Food and Wine Experience are just a couple of the annual festivals held on the island.

It's crucial to prepare ahead of time and be informed of your transportation alternatives when island-hopping in the US Virgin Islands. Making bookings in advance is a smart idea because during high season, flights and ferries can fill up rapidly. Check with your accommodations for possibilities since many hotels and resorts in the USVI offer package deals that include travel to and from other islands.

The US Virgin Islands contain a number of smaller islands and cays that are well worth seeing in addition to the three main islands of St. Thomas, St. John, and St. Croix. A ferry can take you to Water Island, which is a tiny, uninhabited island off the coast of St. Thomas. A lovely beach, as well as a few eateries and pubs, can be found on the island. Another nearby St. Thomas location, Hassel Island, is a historic landmark that can be explored on foot or by kayak. There are many hiking routes on the island, which also provides sweeping views of Charlotte Amalie port.

Renting a sailboat or catamaran is another popular method of getting around by boat in the USVI. Many businesses provide day charters or overnight cruises so that tourists can see the islands' natural beauty from the ocean. When visiting the USVI by boat, snorkeling and diving are common pastimes because the crystal-clear waters are home to a diversity of marine life and coral reefs.

Island hopping is a fantastic way to discover the US Virgin Islands and take in each island's own culture, history, and natural beauty. There is one island in the USVI that is ideal for you, whether your interests include dining, shopping, hiking, or just lounging on the beach. Island hopping in the USVI is likely to be a once-in-a-lifetime experience thanks to the abundance of transportation choices and the range of activities and attractions available.

Chapter 5: Culture and Cuisine

The US Virgin Islands are a cultural melting pot with elements of the Caribbean, Europe, and Africa. This chapter will offer you a taste of the USVI's delectable cuisine as well as its distinctive history and traditions.

USVI Culture and History

The original occupants of the US Virgin Islands were the Ciboney people, who came there approximately 5000 BCE. The USVI have a rich cultural and historical heritage that has been affected by its indigenous peoples and history of colonization. The Taino people arrived shortly after the Ciboney, in the year 300 CE. The Taino people were hunters and fishermen who also farmed crops like cassava and yams. They subsisted off the land and the water. Additionally, they followed a religion that comprised adoration of deities, ancestors, and the natural environment.

The USVI entered a new phase in the late 15th century with the entrance of the Europeans. During his second journey to the Americas, Christopher Columbus saw the islands in 1493 and gave them the names of St. Ursula and her 11,000 virgins. But the Spanish did not remain on the islands long, and it was not until the 17th century that European colonization really got going.

Early in the 17th century, the Dutch were the first to build villages on St. Croix and St. Thomas. Following them came the French, then the Danish, who eventually took control of all three islands and built a successful sugar business using the labor of slaves from Africa.

Thousands of Africans were forcibly taken to the islands to work on sugar plantations, making slavery a significant part of the history of the US Virgin Islands. Long hours, severe penalties, and little to no freedom were all part of the tough working environment. However, the enslaved Africans discovered strategies for resistance and survival, and today, the USVI's culture and identity are still shaped by their descendants.

In 1917, the USVI was purchased by the US, which thereafter claimed the islands as its own territory. The US Virgin Islands (USVI) were an important Allied base for the Navy and Air Force during World War II. The war significantly altered the US Virgin Islands' economy and society, and many islanders fought in the military.

Africa, Europe, and the Caribbean are all represented in the USVI's rich and diversified culture today. Visitors can develop a greater understanding of the USVI's rich cultural and historical heritage and the islands' inhabitants. A great approach to immerse oneself in the intriguing past and present of the USVI is to visit the museums, historic sites, and cultural events.

The Indigenous Peoples of the USVI

Before European explorers arrived, the USVI's first known residents were the Ciboney and Taino peoples, who inhabited the islands for hundreds of years. The original inhabitants were the Ciboney, who are thought to have migrated to the Caribbean islands from South America some 2,500 years ago. They were followed by the Taino people, who arrived after them and brought with them more advanced agricultural and technological practices.

Native inhabitants of the US Virgin Islands relied on farming, fishing, and hunting to survive. Using nets and hooks fashioned of bone and shell, they fished for shellfish, snapper, and other species of fish. In addition, they raised crops like cassava, yams, and maize, as well as hunting iguanas, birds, and small wildlife. The Taino people were adept at carving wood and stone, weaving hammocks and baskets, and making pottery.

The USVI entered a new era with the arrival of Christopher Columbus in the late 15th century. The Spanish explorers who came after Columbus swiftly reduced the native populations to slavery and forced them to labor in mines and farms. Numerous native people perished from disease, cruel treatment, and contact with diseases brought over by Europeans to which they lacked immunity.

The native people on St. Croix had already been wiped out by the time the Dutch came there in the early 17th century. On the island, a trade post was first constructed by the Dutch, then by the French and the Danish. Because of the islands' strategic location, European countries struggled for control of them for centuries.

Through a variety of cultural and educational initiatives, the USVI now pays tribute to the contributions of its indigenous peoples. The Virgin Islands Humanities Council funds events and programs that honor the islands' rich cultural past, and the University of the Virgin Islands provides courses on Caribbean history, culture, and archaeology. By visiting the many historical sites and museums, like the St. Croix Archaeological Society and the Estate Whim Museum on St. Croix, visitors to the USVI can also learn about the indigenous history of the islands.

The Impact of Colonialism on the USVI

The Colonization by the Dutch, French, and Danish:

The Dutch founded a colony on St. Croix in 1625 and were the first Europeans to settle in the USVI. The French arrived to St. Thomas in 1665 and established themselves after them. All three islands were ultimately bought by the Danish, who set up plantations to grow sugar cane, coffee, and other commodities. The Danes relied significantly on enslaved Africans who were transported over from West Africa in great numbers to work on these plantations. Over 20,000 enslaved Africans were living and working on the plantations on the USVI by the early 19th century.

The Slave Trade and the Sugar Industry:

The sugar business in the USVI played a significant role in the colonial economy and was highly dependent on the labor of enslaved Africans. Long hours, difficult labor conditions, and physical torture were commonplace for those who were forced to live as slaves in Africa. Their lives were characterized by pain and exploitation, and many Africans who were enslaved perished from overwork, illness, or mistreatment.

The USVI Today and the Abolition of Slavery:

In the USVI, slavery was outlawed in 1848, and the islands made the transition to a wage labor economy. But up until 1917, when it was ceded to the United States for $25 million, the USVI was still a Danish colony. The islands were made into a U.S. territory, and the USVI is now a thriving and ethnically diverse region with influences from the Caribbean, Europe, and Africa. The US Virgin Islands are still dealing with the effects of colonialism as they struggle with issues of cultural identity, social inequality, and economic progress.

By visiting historical places like the Estate Whim Museum on St. Croix, the Fort Christian Museum on St. Thomas, or the Virgin Islands History Museum on St. John, visitors to the USVI can learn more about the history of the islands. Visitors can gain an understanding of the nuances of the USVI's cultural and historical legacy by visiting these museums, which provide an insight into the colonial past of the islands.

The USVI in the 20th Century

The USVI was vital to the Allied forces during World War II. Many islanders participated in the military since the Navy and Air Force exploited the islands as a strategic station. The USVI was significantly impacted by the military presence, which changed the local economy and brought new residents and resources to the islands.

The USVI saw substantial economic and social upheaval after the war. The islands started a phase of renovation and development with the aid of the federal government. The promotion of new sectors like manufacturing and tourism led to a diversification of the USVI's economy.

One of the most significant sectors in the USVI immediately emerged as tourism. The natural beauty, pleasant climate, and colorful culture of the islands drew tourists. The islands' beaches gained international recognition as a result of the construction of hotels and resorts. Today, the USVI is still a well-liked vacation spot, drawing numerous millions of tourists yearly.

Additionally, the USVI was crucial to the civil rights movement. Local activists campaigned against racial segregation and for equal rights in the 1950s and 1960s. Due to the islands' distinct status as a U.S. territory, the fight for civil rights had to be carried out differently than it would have been on the American mainland. Nevertheless, the USVI was at the vanguard of the struggle for equality thanks to local activists like Vito M. Sewer, an educator, and civil rights attorneys David Hamilton Jackson.

The USVI is a prosperous community with a multiethnic population today. The economy of the islands still depends on tourism as well as on other sectors like finance and healthcare. The USVI has a bright future despite its difficulties thanks to its distinctive combination of history, culture, and natural beauty, which makes it a one-of-a-kind travel destination.

The USVI Today: Language, Art, and Music

Africa, Europe, and the Caribbean are all represented in the USVI's rich and diversified culture today. Although Creole and Spanish are also widely spoken on the island, English is the official language. From the moko jumbies (stilt dancers) to the vivid murals found on buildings around the islands, the USVI is renowned for its rich and expressive art. Calypso, reggae, and steel pan music are just a few examples of the many musical styles that are an integral part of USVI culture.

Visitors can have a greater understanding of the islands and its people by learning about the culture and history of the USVI. To fully experience the USVI's distinctive cultural environment, I recommend visiting the museums, historical landmarks, and art galleries.

Local Cuisine and Dining Recommendations

The US Virgin Islands' cuisine is among the greatest ways to experience the local culture. The USVI is renowned for its savory cuisine, which reflects its lengthy history and wide range of cultural influences. Here are some must-try foods, seafood specialties, and regional beverages, along with suggestions for the top USVI eateries and food trucks.

USVI Food Staples

The typical food of the USVI is substantial, filling, and hearty. The following are some of the most well-liked USVI foodstuffs:

Saltfish: A traditional breakfast food in the US Virgin Islands, saltfish is a local favorite. It is made of salted fish that has been boiled, dipped in water to remove the salt, and served with mushrooms, a side dish made of cornmeal, and a side of spicy sauce. A tasty and filling meal like saltfish will give you the vigor you need to tackle the day.

Johnny Cake: A fluffy bread made of cornmeal known as "Johnny Cake" is frequently consumed for breakfast or as a snack. It frequently goes with butter or jam and can be either sweet or savory. In various eateries and bakeries all around the USVI, you may find johnny cake, a mainstay of Caribbean food.

Callaloo: A sort of leafy green used in stews and soups is called callaloo. It resembles spinach and is nutrient-rich, including iron and vitamins A and C. To make recipes that are tasty and nourishing, callaloo is frequently paired with other ingredients like okra, coconut milk, and fish.

Pate: Pate is a delicious pastry with meat, poultry, fish, or vegetables inside. In the USVI, you can find it at most food trucks or neighborhood bakeries as a popular snack or lunch option. Pate is a fantastic choice for a quick and filling supper on the run and may be had hot or cold.

Roti: The Caribbean is a region that enjoys roti, an Indian flatbread. It frequently comes with a side of chutney and is stuffed with curried meat or veggies. In the US Virgin Islands, roti is a common dish in small eateries and food trucks.
Another popular morning food in the USVI is fish and mushrooms. It consists of fried fish (often snapper or grouper) and fungus, a side dish made of cornmeal that is comparable to polenta.

Conch fritters are a well-liked appetizer in the US Virgin Islands. They are created from flour, spices, and ground conch that has been deep-fried till crispy. They frequently come with an aioli or hot sauce side dish.

Traditional callaloo, okra, pumpkin, and other veggies are used to make kallaloo soup. It is a filling and healthy dish that is frequently served with a side of rice or bread.

Mango, papaya, and passionfruit are just a few of the tropical fruits that may be found on the US Virgin Islands. On a hot day, a chilled fruit salad is a wonderful way to enjoy these fruits.

During your stay to the USVI, you should also taste some of the many additional regional delicacies that are available in addition to these typical cuisine. Mahi-mahi, conch, and lobster are some of the fresh seafood you should eat, as well as Cruzan rum and Bush tea, two regional beverages. You're guaranteed to enjoy an outstanding gastronomic experience in the US Virgin Islands with so many delectable selections to pick from.

Seafood Delicacies

The waters around the US Virgin Islands are home to the popular fish known as mahi-mahi, commonly referred to as dolphinfish or dorado. Due to its solid structure, subtle sweetness, and adaptability in cooking, it is a widely sought-after fish. Frequently eaten with a variety of sides, including rice and beans, plantains, or vegetables, mahi-mahi is frequently grilled, fried, or baked.

Another seafood delicacy popular in the US Virgin Islands and found in the Caribbean is conch. It is a kind of sea snail that is frequently used in soups, stews, and salads because of its tough, chewy texture. Conch is a flexible ingredient that may be used in many different dishes, such as conch fritters and conch salad. Some natives also believe it to be aphrodisiac.

Locals frequently order the Caribbean spiny lobster grilled, broiled, or boiled. It is a preferred option for seafood lovers because of its sweet and soft flavor. The lobster meat goes nicely with sides like rice, veggies, or salad and is frequently served with butter or a sour dipping sauce.

In order to promote sustainability and the preservation of the local ecology, there are stringent laws for lobster fishing in the US Virgin Islands. In order to safeguard the breeding population, it is forbidden to catch lobsters that are smaller than a certain size or during a specific time of the year.

For any foodie or seafood enthusiast, the seafood specialties found in the US Virgin Islands are a must-try. There is something for every palette, whether it is the firm and tasty mahi-mahi, the chewy and adaptable conch, or the sweet and soft Caribbean spiny lobster.

Local Drinks

If you visit the US Virgin Islands, you must sample some of the local libations. Here are a few of the most well-liked local beverages that you ought to try:
Cruzan Rum, a mainstay in the US Virgin Islands, is renowned for its fine quality and pleasant flavor. This rum is created in-country on the island of St. Croix from molasses, a by-product of sugar processing, and is then matured in oak barrels. The rum's distinct flavor profile, which combines vanilla, caramel, and oak, is a result of the aging process. Tropical drinks like the well-known Painkiller, which is mixed with rum, pineapple juice, orange juice, and cream of coconut, frequently feature Cruzan Rum.

Another well-liked local brew that is appreciated by both locals and visitors is bush tea. A combination of regional plants and herbs, including lemongrass, ginger, and soursop, are used to make this herbal tea. It is frequently used to treat a variety of illnesses, from sore throats to unsettled stomachs, and is considered to have healing effects. Additionally, it's a well-liked way to unwind after a long day and is frequently taken before bed.

Locally farmed passion fruit is used to make the sweet and sour liquid known as passion fruit juice. The juice of this delectable fruit is sometimes combined with other fruits to make cool tropical beverages. Its tangy flavor is ideal for hot days. In addition, passion fruit is a common ingredient in drinks like the Hurricane, which is a blend of passion fruit, rum, and other tropical juices. Passion fruit is also used in a range of sweets, including cakes and tarts.

A few examples of the distinctive and delectable flavors that may be found in the US Virgin Islands are these local beverages. There is something to suit everyone's tastes, whether they prefer a tropical cocktail or a refreshing drink. You're also guaranteed to discover new and intriguing flavors to try while you're there thanks to the wealth of fruits and herbs that are cultivated locally.

Best USVI Restaurants and Food Trucks

In the USVI, there are many places to eat, from fast food joints to fine dining establishments. Here are some of the top restaurants in the US Virgin Islands:

Anyone who enjoys Caribbean cuisine must visit Gladys' Cafe in St. Thomas. Since it has been around for more than 30 years, this local landmark has been a beloved hangout for both residents and tourists. The curried goat, oxtail stew, and conch fritters are a few of the things you must try. The restaurant features a courteous staff and a cozy, welcoming ambiance. The design is bright.

For a dinner with a view, head to Cane Bay Beach in St. Croix. Fish tacos, shrimp scampi, and grilled mahi-mahi are just a few of the mouthwatering seafood dishes offered at this beachfront bar and restaurant. Due to the open-air design of the restaurant, customers may enjoy the breathtaking ocean views while they eat. The bar also offers a selection of tropical cocktails, such as pia coladas and margaritas.

Some of the best street cuisine in the USVI is served by Off the Grid, a food truck based in St. John. The tacos, burgers, and sandwiches on the menu are all crafted using fresh, regional ingredients. The food truck features a relaxed ambiance with picnic tables and a vibrant, seaside theme.

Before leaving to tour the island, it's a fantastic place to grab a quick bite.

Intimate and homey, The Twisted Cork Cafe in St. Croix offers a variety of superb wines, delicious sandwiches, and salads. The brie and apple sandwich, pear and arugula salad, and mushroom risotto are just a few of the inventive and delectable meals on the menu. Dim lighting and cozy seats create a cozy and welcoming atmosphere in the restaurant.

Popular bar and eatery Caribbean Saloon in St. Thomas serves delectable seafood, burgers, and sandwiches. Conch fritters and the jerk chicken sandwich are just a couple of the Caribbean-inspired menu items. The pub provides a vibrant environment with music playing late into the night and drinks being served.

Fresh seafood is served at the waterfront restaurant Latitude 18 in St. Thomas, which also features a bustling bar scene. The grilled fish tacos and the coconut shrimp are just two of the excellent meals on the menu. The renowned Painkiller cocktail is among the tropical beverages offered at the bar. The restaurant boasts outside dining with breathtaking seaside views, and the ambiance is relaxed and casual.

In St. John, the relaxed Island Time Pub offers mouthwatering burgers, sandwiches, and salads in addition to a wide range of beer and beverages. The menu features a wide selection of traditional pub fare as well as several items with Caribbean influences, like the jerk chicken sandwich. There is indoor and outdoor seating available in the pub, which has a laid-back and welcoming vibe.

In St. Thomas, the informal eatery Tap and Still serves up delicious burgers and artisan beer. The mac and cheese burger and the blue cheese and bacon burger are just a couple of the tasty and inventive burgers on the menu. Along with a selection of other beverages, the restaurant also serves craft beer. There is both indoor and outdoor sitting available, and the mood is relaxed and casual.

There are several excellent food trucks to select from, and food trucks are a popular eating option in the US Virgin Islands. Tasty tacos and burritos with a range of inventive ingredients and toppings are available from the Loco Gypsy food truck. Delicious burgers and sandwiches are cooked with regional ingredients by the Love City Food Truck. The Tapas Wagon, which offers Spanish-inspired fare, and the Sweet Plantains food truck, which offers Caribbean-inspired desserts, are two further well-known food trucks.

The Fish Trap (St. John) is a family-run eatery that offers delectable fresh fish meals in a warm environment. Try their famed fish tacos or their grilled fish served with a side of plantains.

Coconuts (St. Croix): This seaside eatery specializes on seafood and serves a variety of Caribbean and American meals. Their conch chowder and lobster mac & cheese are not to be missed.

Duffy's Love Shack in St. Thomas offers mouthwatering burgers and cocktails with a tropical flair. For taking in the island wind, the outside seating area is ideal.

Locals love the informal fish eatery Hook, Line & Sinker in St. Croix because it serves up daily fresh catches as well as various seafood dishes. Try the blackened Mahi-Mahi or the fish and chips there.

The Tap Room at Mongoose Junction (St. John) is a restaurant and bar that offers a range of foods like sushi, pizza, and sandwiches. It is situated in a lovely retail area. They also provide a wide variety of craft beers.

Even though it's not a restaurant, St. John Scoops is a must-stop for anyone with a sweet craving. Local favorites like coconut and mango are among the handcrafted ice cream flavors they offer.

The relaxed Island Time Pub in St. John offers mouthwatering burgers, sandwiches, and salads in addition to a wide range of beer and beverages. Both locals and tourists frequent the area.

The rich and varied cuisine of the US Virgin Islands reflects the island's history and cultural influences. There is something for everyone to enjoy, from classic dishes like saltfish and Johnny cake to exquisite seafood dishes like mahi-mahi and conch. Additionally, you are likely to find something that meets your taste and budget among the diversity of dining alternatives available, which range from luxury restaurants to casual food trucks.

Festivals and Events

The US Virgin Islands are renowned for their colorful celebrations and festivals that showcase the islands' distinct culture and past. Listed below are some of the most well-known activities you shouldn't skip while you're in the US Virgin Islands:

Carnival: The USVI's Biggest Party

The most well-known and entertaining event in the US Virgin Islands is Carnival, which is observed on all three islands. In the USVI, Carnival dates back to the 18th century, when Africans who were still in slavery were permitted to revel briefly before Lent. Today, Carnival is the major event on the social calendar of the islands, lasting for several weeks before Easter Sunday.

The two main events are the St. Thomas Carnival and the St. Croix Crucian Christmas Carnival, while the St. John Festival is a relatively low-key occasion. What to expect during Carnival in the USVI is as follows:

Parades

- The most well-liked activities of the festivities are the carnival parades, which are a riot of color, song, and vigor.
- The parades wind through the streets of Charlotte Amalie in St. Thomas and Frederiksted in St. Croix and include extravagant floats, costumed entertainers, and steel drum bands.
- The adults' parade is the focal point of the Crucian Christmas Carnival in St. Croix, while the children's parade, senior citizens' procession, and adults' parade are the primary parades in St. Thomas.

Concerts and Music

- There are a lot of concerts and performances involving both domestic and foreign artists during Carnival, which is a time for music and dancing.
- The steel pan drumming, calypso, soca, and reggae music of the US Virgin Islands is a distinctive fusion of African, European, and Caribbean elements.
- Popular music events during the St. Thomas Carnival include the International Reggae Night and the Latin Night, while the Food, Arts and Crafts Fair and the Calypso Monarch Competition are held during the Crucian Christmas Carnival in St. Croix.

Dancing and Cultural Shows

- Dancing plays a significant role in Carnival, and there are several possibilities to pick up regional dances and compete in dance contests.
- Cultural performances, which highlight the rich history and customs of the USVI, are also significant components of Carnival.

- The Quadrille dancers reflect the European influence on the islands, while the Mocko Jumbies, stilt-walkers who perform during Carnival, are a recognizable representation of the USVI's African past.

Food and Drink

- Carnival is also a chance to indulge in regional cuisine and beverages.
- The US Virgin Islands have a thriving culinary culture that combines African, European, and Caribbean influences. Dishes include anything from lobster and conch fritters to saltfish and johnnycakes.
- Local beverages like Cruzan rum, bush tea, and mauby are especially well-liked during Carnival, and you may buy their products from several food and beverage vendors at the various events.

Indulging in the local culture and traditions by participating in Carnival in the USVI is a memorable experience. Booking your lodging well in advance is advised because Carnival is a popular time to visit the islands. Also, remember to bring your dancing shoes!

St. Croix Food and Wine Experience

In the US Virgin Islands, one of the most well-liked food festivals is the St. Croix Food and Wine Experience. This annual celebration of the local food and wine scene lasts for a full week in April and features a wide range of activities for fans of both.

Tastings and Cooking Demonstrations:

- The Taste of St. Croix event, where guests may taste the island's top foods and beverages from local restaurants, chefs, and vendors, serves as the official start of the St. Croix Food and Wine Experience.

- Throughout the week, there are also wine tastings and food demos where you can learn how to make new wines and vintages, as well as cooking classes where you can learn how to prepare and cook regional dishes.
- Wine Dinners and Seminars
- The St. Croix Food and Wine Experience also offers a number of wine seminars and dinners where you can find out more about various varietals and pairings and get a chance to interact with famous winemakers and sommeliers.
- You may enjoy a multi-course meal paired with wines from all over the world at the wine dinners, which are held at some of the island's most prominent restaurants.
- Discover Renowned Winemakers and Chefs
- Meeting and interacting with well-known chefs and winemakers from all over the world is one of the highlights of the St. Croix Food and Wine Experience.
- The festival draws some of the most well-known figures in the wine and culinary industries, who frequently take part in the many events and seminars and share their knowledge and experiences.

Many neighborhood restaurants and bars also provide special menus and activities throughout the festival in addition to the official St. Croix Food and Wine Experience events, making it a fantastic time to discover the island's culinary culture. The St. Croix Food and Wine Experience is a unique opportunity that shouldn't be missed while you're in the US Virgin Islands, whether you're a foodie or a wine connoisseur.

Crucian Christmas Festival

In the US Virgin Islands, the Crucian Christmas Festival is a well-liked celebration that is the ideal way to get into the holiday spirit. The event has been observed for more than 60 years and is exclusive to the island of St. Croix. Here are a some of the festival's high points:
Family and Community

- Families and friends can join together during the Crucian Christmas Festival to celebrate the holiday season.
- The event is firmly entrenched in the neighborhood and provides a chance for residents and guests to interact and get a taste of the local way of life.
- food and beverage
- In the USVI, no celebration would be complete without delectable food and a chance to sample regional beverages like rum punch.

Dance and music

- Live performances by neighborhood musicians and dancers are a key component of the Crucian Christmas Festival.
- Various musical genres, such as reggae, soca, calypso, and steelpan, are featured at the festival.
- Participants in dancing workshops can pick up classic dances like the quadrille and cariso.

Pageants and parades

- The Crucian Christmas Festival includes a number of pageants and parades, such as the Food Fair Parade, Adult Parade, and Children's Parade.

- Thousands of onlookers flock to watch the parades, which are filled with vibrant floats, traditional costumes, and upbeat music.
- Local talent is showcased in the pageants in categories including Miss St. Croix and Mr. Umoja.

Three Kings Day Parade

- The Three Kings Day Parade, which takes place on January 6, is the centerpiece of the Crucian Christmas Festival.
- The procession honors the Three Wise Men's arrival and includes vibrant floats, ethnic attire, and regional music.

The parade begins at dawn and concludes at the Frederiksted Pier with a customary bull and horse racing.

You won't want to miss the Crucian Christmas Festival because it is a memorable event. It's a wonderful chance to become immersed in the customs and culture of the area and to spend the holiday season with the hospitable residents of St. Croix.

Other Festivals and Celebrations

The St. John Festival

Every year in June, the island of St. John hosts the St. John Festival, a month-long festival. Visitors from all over the world come to the festival, one of the biggest on the island, to take in the unique culture and customs of the US Virgin Islands.

The festival offers a variety of performances, parades, concerts, culinary markets, beauty pageants, and cultural displays. These gatherings offer guests a special chance to get a taste of the dynamic musical, dancing, and culinary traditions of St. John while showcasing the island's rich cultural legacy.

The St. John Festival's Grand Parade, which happens on the festival's last day, is one of its highlights. The Grand Parade is a vibrant and animated procession that travels through Cruz Bay, the major settlement on the island. The parade is a sight to behold and involves ornately painted floats, energetic musical acts, and costumed dancers.

There are numerous other events and activities throughout the festival, in addition to the Grand Parade, that are certain to excite attendees of all ages. There are also cultural performances that highlight St. John's rich history and traditions, beauty pageants that display the island's best performers, and food markets that serve regional Caribbean cuisine.

In addition to the Grand Parade, the St. John Festival offers access to several parades. The Children's Parade, which occurs a few days before the Grand Parade, is one of them. Children dressed in vibrant costumes and floats with decorations are included in the Children's Parade, which is entertaining and family-friendly. Children have a wonderful opportunity to participate in the event and learn about US Virgin Islands culture.

The Food Fair is yet another popular St. John Festival activity. The Food Fair is a fantastic place to try authentic Caribbean food and take in the neighborhood's culinary scene. Visitors can sample new flavors and foods while taking in the joyful atmosphere at the fair, which has a range of food booths selling anything from savory meat dishes to sweet desserts.

The St. John Festival also offers a variety of musical concerts and shows for music fans. These include contemporary pop and rock acts as well as classic Caribbean musical genres like calypso and reggae. While taking in the excitement and spirit of the event, attendees can sing and dance to the music.
The St. John Festival honors St. John and the US Virgin Islands' vibrant cultural heritage. The festival gives attendees the chance to take in the finest of Caribbean music, cuisine, and culture in a fun and festive setting through its many events and activities.

The St. Thomas International Regatta

One of the most thrilling and eagerly awaited occasions in the US Virgin Islands, the St. Thomas International Regatta attracts sailors and spectators from all over the world. Here are some more specifics about this thrilling occasion:

The Races:

- The St. Thomas International Regatta features three days of competition on several courses that are intended to challenge and test the sailors' abilities.
- With fluctuating wind and current conditions, the race courses often combine buoy racing and point-to-point racing.
- From novice cruisers to experienced racers, a variety of boats and sailing aficionados are welcome to participate in the regatta.

The Social Events:

- The St. Thomas International Regatta offers a variety of entertaining and dynamic social events in addition to the thrilling races.
- Social events, such as live music performances, food and drink sellers, and beach parties, bring together sailors, spectators, and residents every evening of the race.
- The event concludes with an awards presentation, when the champions of the various races are honored.

Getting Involved:

- Everyone may participate in and enjoy the excitement of the St. Thomas International Regatta; it is not just for seasoned sailors.
- Spectators can take part in the many social activities and celebrations as well as observe the races from the shore or from a spectator boat.
- There are options to crew on a racing boat or even take part in the races themselves for individuals who are interested in sailing.

People from all over the world come together for the St. Thomas International Regatta to celebrate their passion of sailing and to take in the stunning Caribbean waters. Here are some more specifics regarding the occasion:

History:

- One of the oldest and most enduring regattas in the Caribbean, the St. Thomas International Regatta has been hosted every year since 1974.

- The event's size and popularity have increased over time, drawing sailors from nations including the United States, Canada, France, Germany, and others.

Location:

- The St. Thomas International Regatta is held in the stunning waters that surround the island of St. Thomas, which make for the perfect sailing environment.
- The St. Thomas Yacht Club serves as the focal point for the event's many races, social gatherings, and celebrations.

Sustainability:

- The St. Thomas International Regatta is dedicated to advancing environmental preservation and sustainability.
- The event promotes eco-friendly boating habits like decreasing carbon emissions, recycling, and waste production.
- In addition, the regatta provides funding to a number of environmental groups and projects in the US Virgin Islands, assisting in the preservation of the islands' natural beauty for future generations.

Overall, the St. Thomas International Regatta is a fun and thrilling occasion that caters to all interests. There are countless opportunities to enjoy the distinct culture and energy of the US Virgin Islands, from the excitement of the races to the fun and colorful social events. The regatta is a must-see event that should be on every traveler's schedule, regardless of whether they are seasoned sailors or first-time visitors.

The St. Croix Agricultural and Food Fair

Anyone traveling to the US Virgin Islands in February must attend the St. Croix Agricultural and Food Fair. This yearly event, which has been organized for more than 40 years, honors the island's rich agricultural tradition and offers tourists a special chance to discover the local foods and products.

The fair offers a wide variety of agriculturally related exhibits, performances, and competitions. Visitors can explore the various crops that are farmed on the island, observe livestock demonstrations, and learn about conventional agricultural practices. The fair also has cooking competitions, wherein home cooks and regional chefs compete to produce the greatest dishes utilizing materials found locally.

The fair's culinary booths, where guests may try a range of locally grown foods and classic recipes, are one of its highlights. The food at the St. Croix Agricultural and Food Fair is a feast for the senses, with locally grown fruits and vegetables as well as freshly caught seafood. Additionally, tourists can buy local goods like rum, honey, and spices to take home with them.

The fair offers live music performances, carnival rides, and other entertainment in addition to the agricultural exhibits and food vendors. There are plenty of opportunities to learn about the history and culture of the island, as well as kid-friendly activities like pony rides and petting zoos.

The St. Croix Agricultural and Food Fair offers attendees the chance to learn more about the island's agricultural heritage. Agriculture has been practiced in the US Virgin Islands for a very long period, ever since the Taino people who lived there originally. Christopher Columbus discovered the island to be covered in thick forests and home to a prosperous agricultural community when he landed in the area in the late 15th century.

Agriculture on the island has developed throughout the years to now include crops including cotton, sugar cane, and coffee. The island now supports a wide range of crops, including goats, sheep, and fruits and vegetables including mangoes, papayas, and callaloo.

Visitors get a rare opportunity to learn about these crops and the methods used to grow them at the St. Croix Agricultural and Food Fair. On-site experts are available to respond to inquiries and share knowledge on everything from planting and harvesting to cooking and preserving.

The expo offers a chance to help the regional agricultural sector. Visitors can support the local economy by purchasing goods from the fair's many local farmers and producers, who also serve as merchants and exhibitors.

The St. Croix Agricultural and Food Fair, in sum, is a distinctive and fascinating occasion that honors the agricultural history of the US Virgin Islands. The fair is a must-visit for anybody interested in gastronomy, history, or culture because it offers a wide variety of exhibitions, demonstrations, and activities. The fair is a fantastic chance to learn about the island's agricultural traditions and support the regional farming sector, whether you're a local or a guest.

The Transfer Day Centennial

The US Virgin Islands celebrated the 100th anniversary of the transfer of the islands from Denmark to the United States with the Transfer Day Centennial, a historic occasion.

The transfer, which happened on March 31, 1917, had a profound effect on the islands' political, economic, and social climate.

The US Virgin Islands' centennial celebration, which took place in March 2017, was a significant occasion that brought residents and guests together to remember this significant historical event. The celebration included a variety of cultural activities and events that highlighted the rich cultural legacy of the islands, such as parades, concerts, historical reenactments, and exhibits for children.

The Centennial Parade, which featured marching bands, dance groups, and vibrant floats, was one of the event's highlights. The procession, which made its way through St. Thomas's streets, served as a visual depiction of the islands' rich cultural legacy.
Another important component of the celebration was the Centennial Village, which offered a variety of cultural displays and activities. Through interactive displays, historical reenactments, and educational events, visitors could learn about the history of the US Virgin Islands.

There were numerous concerts and musical events throughout the festival, featuring both domestic and foreign performers. These occasions offered a rare chance to take part in the vivid music and dancing customs of the US Virgin Islands.

The Transfer Day Centennial commemoration offered a chance to acknowledge and pay tribute to the contributions made by those who have shaped the history of the US Virgin Islands. Both the indigenous peoples who first lived on the islands and the African slaves who were brought there to work on sugar plantations are included in this.

The commemoration of the 100th anniversary also brought attention to the continued battles and difficulties that the US Virgin Islands are currently facing, including problems with economic development, political representation, and environmental sustainability. The event urged attendees to consider the future of the islands critically and to look for solutions through a number of educational events and exhibitions.

The heightened interest in the history and culture of the US Virgin Islands has been one of the Transfer Day Centennial's enduring legacies. Since the celebration, there has been more money invested in heritage tourism and cultural preservation, as well as initiatives to advertise the islands' distinctive cultural identity on a global scale.

The US Virgin Islands' rich cultural legacy and complicated history were highlighted by the Transfer Day Centennial, which was a landmark occasion in the islands' history. These festivals and celebrations offer a distinctive opportunity to experience the culture and history of the US Virgin Islands. Through a variety of cultural events and activities, the celebration brought locals and visitors together to reflect on the past, celebrate the present, and look towards the future. There is something for everyone to enjoy, regardless of your interests in music, food, sports, or history. To get the most out of your stay, be sure to review the event schedules and make travel arrangements appropriately.

There are a few additional events and festivals in the US Virgin Islands that tourists might find interesting:

1. Three Kings Day: In the US Virgin Islands, this Christian feast is observed on January 6. The occasion is a wonderful way to learn about the island's rich cultural heritage and is

celebrated with parades, music, food, and other cultural activities.

2. Carnival Village: Many US Virgin Islands communities erect a Carnival Village prior to Carnival. In the weeks preceding the main Carnival event, these outdoor venues host food sellers, musical and dance performances, and other cultural events.

3. Every Thursday, there is an event called "Art Thursday" in St. Thomas and St. John. Many of the island's art galleries stay open late on Thursdays, allowing guests to admire local artists' creations and enjoy free refreshments.

4. Jazz in the Park: In Charlotte Amalie, St. Thomas, there is a monthly event called Jazz in the Park. The historic Emancipation Garden will have live jazz music performances during the occasion, along with food vendors and other cultural pursuits.

5. The Latin Festival is a yearly celebration that takes place in St. Croix. The festival showcases Latin music and dance acts, as well as food vendors and other Hispanic heritage-related cultural events.

A wonderful way to get a taste of the local customs, cuisine, and culture is to take part in one of the US Virgin Islands' festivals or celebrations. To truly experience the vibrant culture of the USVI, be sure to check the festival schedules and plan your vacation appropriately.

You can genuinely enjoy the native way of life and feel more connected to the islands if you are aware of the culture and cuisine of the USVI. Don't pass up the chance to sample some regional specialties and take part in one of the many festivals that honor the USVI's distinctive history.

Chapter 6: Practical Information

It's crucial to be aware of practical information that can make your vacation to the US Virgin Islands easier and more enjoyable. We discuss money and budgeting, safety and health, communication and internet access, as well as helpful language and phrases, in this chapter.

Money and Budgeting

Currency:
The US dollar is the official currency in the US Virgin Islands. This entails that visitors from the US don't have to bother about exchanging money and can use their dollars as they choose. Despite the fact that credit cards are frequently accepted on the islands, it is still advisable to have some cash on hand for smaller purchases like buying products from street vendors or tipping.

Budgeting:
The US Virgin Islands can be quite pricey, especially if you stay at one of the upscale resorts or eat at fine dining establishments. There are still many ways to save money while taking advantage of everything the islands have to offer, though.

In the US Virgin Islands, consider the following financial advice:

Accommodation:
The US Virgin Islands have a selection of lodging choices, from opulent resorts to inexpensive guesthouses and vacation rentals. A guesthouse or vacation rental can be a

wonderful choice if you're trying to save money. These alternatives not only tend to be less expensive than resorts, but they also allow you a chance to immerse yourself deeper in the local way of life. Since many vacation rentals are owned and managed by locals, you can obtain insider knowledge on the top restaurants and activities.

Dining:
In the US Virgin Islands, eating out can be costly, particularly at eateries that cater to tourists. Eat at neighborhood restaurants and food trucks to reduce your food costs. You'll not only save money, but you'll also get to sample real regional cuisine. Conch fritters, fried plantains, and johnnycakes are a few of the local cuisine's most well-liked specialties. Additionally, you can reduce your meal prices by purchasing drinks and snacks at supermarkets. You can stock up on necessities like water and snacks at supermarkets, which are frequently far more economical than dining establishments or quick-service establishments.

Transportation:
Although they are offered in the US Virgin Islands, cabs might be pricey. If you want to cut costs on transportation, think about using the bus or renting a car. Buses travel frequently over the islands and are both inexpensive and simple to use. The buses are referred to as "safaris" and are typically open-air trucks or vans that are painted brightly with enjoyable themes. They're an excellent way to get to know locals and tour the islands. If you want to explore the islands independently, renting a car can be a smart alternative, especially if you're going in a group.

Activities:
The US Virgin Islands provide a wide variety of free or inexpensive activities. The islands are renowned for having stunning beaches, and many of the better ones are open to

the public for no charge. Magens Bay on St. Thomas, Cinnamon Bay on St. John, and Frederiksted Beach on St. Croix are a few examples of well-liked beaches. In addition, there are several free or inexpensive hiking routes and other outdoor activities. For instance, the 72-mile St. Croix Heritage Trail passes through some of the island's most beautiful landscapes. Additionally, you can go to historical places like the Whim Plantation Museum in St. Croix or the Fort Christian Museum on St. Thomas.

You can take use of these cost-effective choices to take advantage of everything the US Virgin Islands has to offer without going overboard.

Health and Safety

Crime
Although it is typically safe to travel to the US Virgin Islands, travellers should nevertheless use caution and common sense. There have been larceny, robberies, and violent crimes in the USVI, where crime rates are greater than the US national average.

It's crucial to be aware of your surroundings and take safety precautions when visiting the US Virgin Islands, such as not carrying significant quantities of cash or valuables, avoiding specific neighborhoods, and never traveling alone at night. Avoid remote beaches or parks and stay in regions that are well-lit. Additionally, it's a good idea to secure your hotel room and place valuables in the hotel safe or safety deposit box.

Report any crimes you are the victim of right away to the local police or your embassy if you are in the US Virgin Islands. 911 should be dialed in case of an emergency in the USVI.

Health

Although the US Virgin Islands have excellent medical services, expenses can be exorbitant. Make sure your travel insurance includes emergency medical evacuation coverage in case it becomes necessary. Additionally, it's a good idea to pack insect repellent, sunscreen, and any essential prescription medications.

In order to protect your skin from the sun's rays when visiting the US Virgin Islands, wear a hat, sunglasses, and sunscreen. Insect repellent should be used, and long sleeves and pants should be worn whenever possible, as mosquitoes can also be a nuisance, particularly during the rainy season (June to November). Take steps to avoid mosquito bites because the USVI has a risk of dengue fever and other diseases transmitted by mosquitoes.

Although drinking the tap water in the USVI is typically safe, many tourists choose to stay with bottled water. If you choose to drink tap water, be warned that it might not taste exactly how you're used to.

Call 911 for assistance if you have a medical emergency while visiting the US Virgin Islands. The Roy Lester Schneider Hospital on St. Thomas, the Governor Juan F. Luis Hospital on St. Croix, and the Myrah Keating Smith Community Health Center on St. John are just a few of the hospitals and medical facilities spread out across the islands.

You may have a safe and healthy trip to the stunning US Virgin Islands by following these safety and health precautions.

Communication and Internet Access

Phone and Internet:
The majority of US Virgin Islands hotels, resorts, and eateries provide free Wi-Fi, and the islands typically have strong cellular coverage. However, it's crucial to clarify with your mobile provider that your plan covers international roaming because costs can be high. If you need to make phone calls, you might think about utilizing a VoIP service like Skype, WhatsApp, or Viber. These services let you make voice and video conversations over the internet for free or at a minimal fee. The purchase of a local SIM card from one of the island's cellular service providers is an additional choice that may come with more reasonable call and data use charges.

Postal Service:
The US Virgin Islands are served by the US Postal Service, and mail is typically delivered to residences and businesses on the islands. It's crucial to anticipate longer delivery times, nevertheless, given the distance and difficulties involved in shipping goods to and from the mainland. For instance, first-class mail from the mainland could take up to five days to arrive, while priority mail could take up to three days. For shipments to or from the US Virgin Islands, several shipping firms may also impose extra fees. It's wise to always confirm delivery dates and any additional costs with your shipping provider or the US Postal Service.

In some of the more inhabited parts of the US Virgin Islands, there may be internet cafes and computer rental stores in addition to Wi-Fi and cellular connectivity. If you need to print boarding passes or check emails but don't have access to a computer or printer, these can be a suitable alternative.

Before making a reservation, be sure your accommodations have reliable internet if you intend to work remotely while on vacation. It could be challenging to operate productively in some lodgings and vacation rentals because of their constrained bandwidth or sporadic internet connectivity.

It's important to keep in mind that some postal deliveries may be subject to additional customs duties or taxes upon arrival in the US Virgin Islands. It's crucial to examine these costs in advance and account for them in your budget if you're transporting goods to the islands.

Finally, it's crucial to pack the proper power adapters and chargers if you intend to travel with electrical equipment like computers, smartphones, or cameras. You won't need to pack any additional converters if you're traveling from the US since the US Virgin Islands use the same voltage and plug types as the US mainland (120V, type A and B plugs). To prevent your electronics from being harmed, you must pack the proper adaptor or converter if you are traveling from a country with a different voltage or plug type.

You can make sure that your trip to the US Virgin Islands runs smoothly and without any hassles by doing some research and making advance plans for communication and internet access.

Local Vocabulary:
You might not be familiar with the lexicon or culture of the US Virgin Islands. Your ability to communicate with people and fully immerse oneself in the culture can be improved by learning a few native words and phrases. Here are a few typical expressions:

- Limin' is a phrase used frequently in the USVI to refer to lounging, unwinding, and enjoying life. It is a way of life on the islands and exemplifies the carefree outlook that many residents enjoy.
- Mauby: This regional beverage is created from tree bark and tastes sweet and a little bit harsh. It's a favorite among locals and a cool beverage to have on a hot day.
- Fungi: A staple of USVI cuisine, this delicacy is made from cornmeal. It is frequently served as a side dish and resembles grits or polenta in texture.
- West Indian: A person from the Caribbean is referred to as such. The US Virgin Islands are in the West Indies, and a large portion of the population considers themselves to be West Indian.

Additionally to improving your ability to converse with the locals, learning a few local words and phrases can demonstrate your sincere interest in US Virgin Islands culture. Asking locals about their language and culture is never a bad idea because they are typically willing to share their knowledge with tourists.

It's also crucial to keep in mind that although English is the main language used in the USVI, Spanish is still widely used, particularly by those employed in the hospitality and service sectors. As a result, if you speak Spanish, you might be able to converse to some locals in their language.

It's also important to note that the US Virgin Islands accept credit cards widely and that the US dollar is their official currency. But it's always a good idea to have cash on hand, especially if you want to travel to smaller stores or markets.

Finally, it's critical to respect regional culture and traditions. For instance, when visiting churches or other places of worship, dress modestly, and take off your shoes before entering someone's home. Additionally, keep in mind that the USVI is a generally conservative region where outward demonstrations of affection are discouraged.

Finally, it might substantially improve your vacation experience if you have a basic familiarity of the US Virgin Islands' language and culture. You may converse with locals more easily and demonstrate that you are genuinely interested in their culture by learning a few basic phrases and vocabulary. Additionally, you can make sure that your trip to this lovely Caribbean location is memorable and delightful by respecting the local customs.

You'll be more prepared for your vacation to the US Virgin Islands if you keep in mind these useful suggestions, and you'll be able to concentrate on taking in all the natural beauty and rich culture that these islands have to offer.

Packing List

It's crucial to pack for the tropical environment and the activities you have planned if you're traveling to the US Virgin Islands. To get you going, here is a list of things to pack:

Pack lightweight, breathable clothing made of natural fibers, such as cotton or linen. Comfortable clothing is essential because the US Virgin Islands have a tropical climate with normal temperatures in the mid-70s to mid-80s Fahrenheit (24–30 degrees Celsius). Additionally, wearing light-colored clothing will keep you cooler outside.

Sun protection: A hat, sunscreen, and sunglasses are necessary for sun protection. Due to the proximity of the equator to the USVI, where the sun can be powerful, it is crucial to take protective measures to prevent skin cancer and sunburns. Select a sunscreen with a high SPF and reapply frequently, especially if you'll be in the water a lot.

Water shoes can assist keep your feet safe while swimming or snorkeling because many of the beaches in the USVI include rocky or coral-filled regions. They can be used on treks or other outdoor activities and offer good traction for walking on slick rocks.

If you intend to snorkel, think about carrying your own equipment, such as a snorkel, mask, and fins. Although some beaches offer rentals, owning your own equipment guarantees a better fit and can ultimately save you money. You won't want to pass up the opportunity to explore the undersea world because the USVI features some of the top snorkeling and diving locations in the Caribbean.

Use insect repellent: Mosquitoes and other insects can be bothersome, especially from May through November when it rains. Consider packing insect repellent and dressing in long sleeves and slacks in the evening to ward off mosquitoes.

Even though the USVI is famed for its mild weather, at night it can get chilly, especially if you're close to the water. Bring a light jacket or sweater. For those chilly evenings, pack a light jacket or sweater, and if you intend to go on a sunset cruise or night trek, pack a light jacket to be warm.

Water bottle: In the humid climate, it's crucial to stay hydrated. Bring a reusable water bottle that you can fill up at drinking fountains or at your hotel. Avoid consuming tap water and, if at all feasible, choose bottled or purified water instead.

Camera: The USVI is a stunning location with lots of photo chances. To record your memories, bring a camera or your smartphone. You won't want to pass up the opportunity to capture images of the vibrant marine life, gorgeous beaches, and spectacular sunsets.

Cash is always a smart option, even though credit cards are commonly used. You can use it for tips, little purchases, or locations that don't accept credit cards. Major credit cards are accepted and US dollars are dispensed by the majority of ATMs in the USVI.

Passports, tickets, and any other necessary travel documentation should not be forgotten. A government-issued ID, such as a driver's license, is always a good idea to bring with you just in case. If you're a US citizen, you won't need a passport to travel to the USVI. Make sure to research the necessary visas if you are coming from another nation.

Useful Websites and Apps

There are several websites and apps that can help you organize your vacation and make the most of your time on the US Virgin Islands if you're thinking about going there. Here are a few that are helpful:

USVI Tourism Website: If you're planning a trip to the islands, the official USVI Tourism Board website is a great place to start. Along with useful details like admittance requirements and transit choices, it provides information on lodging, dining, events, and activities. Additionally, the website contains a "Plan Your Trip" area that offers first-time visitors helpful hints and information, along with suggested itineraries and suggestions for things to do.

Google Maps: If you need help finding your way around the US Virgin Islands, Google Maps is a great resource. It can be used to locate specific areas, get driving instructions, and even find new places to travel to. If you don't have access to

Wi-Fi or mobile data, the app also features a feature that lets you download maps for offline use.

TripAdvisor: TripAdvisor is a well-known travel website that offers reviews and rankings of lodging, dining establishments, and attractions submitted by users. You can use it to browse reviews left by other visitors and obtain suggestions for the top USVI tourist attractions. Additionally, the website features a booking tool that enables you to schedule lodging, excursions, and other activities.

OpenTable: If you want to reserve a table for dinner while you're traveling, this helpful software lets you check up restaurants and book appointments online. You can look for restaurants depending on their location, menu, and price range. You can also read reviews left by previous customers.

My Virgin Islands App: This software, called My Virgin Islands, was created especially for travelers to the US Virgin Islands. It contains details about the islands' beaches, eateries, events, and other activities. Along with a map tool that lets you navigate the islands and make plans, the app also offers a helpful "Near Me" feature that displays attractions and sites of interest close by.

Airbnb: If you're seeking for different lodging options when traveling, this well-known software lets you reserve vacation rentals from nearby owners. In addition to reading reviews from previous visitors, you may search for properties based on your preferred area and spending limit. If you're traveling in a group or seeking a more authentic local experience, Airbnb can be a fantastic alternative.

NOAA Weather App: The US Virgin Islands are susceptible to tropical storms and hurricanes, particularly during the summer. During your vacation, the NOAA Weather App is a helpful resource for staying informed about the most recent weather conditions and alerts. The app offers real-time information on weather conditions, including hurricane warnings and notifications for severe weather.

VI Taxi App: The US Virgin Islands' VI Taxi App offers a practical way to reserve and pay for cabs. The app pairs you with a certified taxi driver after you choose your pickup location, destination, and chosen payment method. The entire process is quick and simple because you can use the app to pay for your transport and track your driver's whereabouts in real-time.

BVI Now App: The BVI Now App is a useful tool for trip planning if you intend to visit the British Virgin Islands while visiting the US Virgin Islands. The app offers details on how to get about, where to stay, where to eat, and what to do in the British Virgin Islands. You may plan your day trips to the BVI and view the most recent ferry timetable feature on the website.

WhatsApp: WhatsApp is a well-known messaging program that can be helpful for connecting with loved ones back home as well as for interacting with locals while you're on vacation. As WhatsApp is widely used by inhabitants in the US Virgin Islands as their main messaging service, using it while traveling can be a practical option.

Uber and Lyft: These ridesharing services, which offer an alternative to standard taxis, are both accessible in the US Virgin Islands. Similar to the VI Taxi App, you may use these applications to order a ride and pay your fare. Remember that in some sections of the islands, availability may be restricted, so it's a good idea to have a backup mode of transportation.

Visitors visiting the US Virgin Islands can have a more enjoyable and stress-free trip by using these websites and apps. There are resources available to help you make the most of your trip to this lovely Caribbean location, whether you're wanting to organize your itinerary, traverse the islands, or remain in touch with loved ones.

Conclusion

In conclusion, every visitor should put the US Virgin Islands on their bucket list because they are such a spectacular place. The USVI offers something for everyone with its magnificent beaches, pristine waters, and rich history and culture.

Each island has its own distinct personality and attractions, from the quaint alleys of Christiansted in St. Croix to the spectacular splendor of Trunk Bay in St. John. The USVI offers a variety of activities, including beach relaxation, historical site exploration, and native food.

You now have all the knowledge you require to organize your ideal trip to the US Virgin Islands thanks to this travel guide. We have you covered with everything from useful advice on finances and transportation to thorough suggestions on where to stay and what to do.

But this guide does more than merely provide knowledge; it also promotes ethical and eco-friendly travel. To have a good impact when traveling, we advise you to support regional companies, protect the environment, and interact with the community.

So why are you still waiting? Prepare for a genuinely unique island holiday by starting to plan your trip to the US Virgin Islands immediately. In this Caribbean paradise, whether it's your first visit or your tenth, there's always something new to discover.

Made in United States
North Haven, CT
04 July 2023

38557847R00095